The Fire and the Knife
And Other Sermons that Matter

Cheryl A. Gosa

Parson's Porch Books
www.parsonsporchbooks.com

The Fire and the Knife and Other Sermons that Matter
ISBN: Softcover 978-1-949888-55-3
Copyright © 2019 by Cheryl A. Gosa

All rights reserved. No part of this book may be reproduced or transmitted in any form or by any means, electronic or mechanical, including photocopying, recording, or by any information storage and retrieval system, without permission in writing from the publisher.

Cover Credit: Abraham Sacrificing Isaac Window in Corona Chapel, Canterbury Cathedral, Canterbury, United Kingdom.

DEDICATION

For Beth, again, and for Elizabeth – both of whom have been with me all the way!

And for the wonderful people at the First Presbyterian Church of Atlanta who have supported and encouraged me through the years - some of whom continue to do so today!

Contents

Sermons Matter 7

Preface 9

The Fire and The Knife 11
    Genesis 22:1-14; Psalm 13

What Lies Ahead 22
    Philippians 3:1-14

Garlands and Jewels 26
    Isaiah 61:1-4, 8-11; I Thess. 5:16-24

One Fine Day 30
    Isaiah 25:6-10

The Unexpected Life 34
    John 3:1-9 34

The Last Laugh 38
    Mark 5:21-43

Full Moon over Managua 42
    Ephesians 2:11-22

Imitators of God 50
    Ephesians 4:25-5:2

The Party's (Almost) Over 54
    John 2:1-12

The Luck of the Irish 59
    Isaiah 58; John 7:37-39

Two Mosquitoes in Tokyo 64
    John 12:1-8; Psalm 36

Into the Night 68
    John 13:21-38; Psalm 88

A Double Share 76
    II Kings 2:1-14; Luke 9:51-62

Holy Ground 86
    Exodus 1:22-2:10, 3:1-5; John 20:11-16,18a

Secret Heart 93
    Psalm 51

The Feast of Humanity 102
    Colossians 1:9-17, 25-29

Floating in Black of Night 111
    Philippians 4:4-6; Isaiah 12:3

Clear as Crystal 114
    Revelation 21: 10-11, 22-26, 22:1-20

Mistletoe, Mist and Dreams 120
    1 Samuel 3: 2 Thessalonians 1:11- 12

Let the Little Children Come 127
    Mark 10:13-16

The River of Life 130
    Genesis 49:1, 29-50:3; Matthew 24:38-44

Finding Our Way Home 135
    Acts 2:41-47

Landscapes and Highways 141
    Acts 9:1-9

Behind the Curtain 146
    Hebrews 6:19

The Good Treasure 150
    Lamentations 3:19-26; II Timothy 1:1-14

The Little Guy 155
    Luke 19:1-10

Snow Village 159
    Isaiah 2:1-4

Testing God 163
    Exodus 17:1-7

Sermons Matter

Parson's Porch Books is delighted to present to you this series called *Sermons Matter*.

We believe that many of the best writers are pastors who take the role of preacher seriously. Week in, and week out, they exegete scripture, research material, write and deliver sermons in the context of the life of their particular congregation in their given community.

We further believe that sermons are extensions of Holy Scripture which need to be published beyond the manuscripts which are written for delivery each Sunday. Books serve as a vehicle for the sermon to continue to proclaim the Good News of the Morning to a broader audience.

Cheryl Gosa provides us with sermons which challenge our minds and warm our heart with insight and the skill of a seasoned preacher.

We celebrate the wonderful occasion of the preaching event in Christian worship when the Pastor speaks, the People listen and the Work of the Church proceeds.

Take, Read, and Heed.

David Russell Tullock, M.Div., D.Min.
Publisher
Parson's Porch Books

Preface

Sermons are designed to speak to people about God on the occasion when they are preached. They are distillations of hours of reading, thinking, studying and prayer. Scholarly work is done in the background to get to the heart of the matter and then that work is converted into words that speak to a specific group of people on a specific occasion.

Candler School of Theology Professor and master preacher, Dr. Fred Craddock, always taught that a sermon should be readily understood by a child with adults listening in, so sometimes a sermon seems too simple and colloquial. A good preacher will make a point through illustrations and after explaining a scripture passage will get to the end with a wrap up pulling it all together and giving the listeners something to take home and chew over as they think about what they heard. If a preacher is lucky, a phrase or an idea will stick and make a difference in a life. That is the work of the Holy Spirit.

Like a diamond or a prism, every scripture passage is the word of God but it can be interpreted over and over by not only different preachers but by the same preacher at different points in her career. That is one of the wonders and the astonishment of lectionary preaching which I always did. To take an assigned passage and find a way to make it relevant today for this group is the magic of preaching.

My seminary professor, Dr. Catherine Gunsalus Gonzalez, at Columbia Theological Seminary, always taught us that every scripture passage can be developed into a communion mediation. I remember the first time I heard that, I thought she could not possibly be right, but over time I have found that indeed, all of the Bible is about coming to the table.

When I was on the pastoral staff at the First Presbyterian Church of Atlanta during the 1990's we had a large staff and a senior minister who liked to preach and to bring in guest preachers. Consequently, we each had one Sunday a year - maybe two if you were willing to take the Sunday after Christmas or the one after Easter - to preach from the pulpit in the beautiful and vast sanctuary.

I wanted to know what it felt like to preach on a regular basis as most Associate Pastors and Solo Pastors do, to be forced to think and pray and study and contemplate every week. So my solution was to negotiate with the senior minister to preach once a month in the chapel where a weekly early morning communion service was held. It was a 30-minute service including the Lord's Supper, so the homily was short. I thrived on this regularity and approached it as something to do on a planned basis. The Senior Minister, Dr. George Wirth, graciously allowed me to name the Sundays I wanted, based on my schedule (I had a young child at the time) and so I knew over a year of Sundays when I was going to be the chapel preacher. I could plan out the sermons accordingly and think and pray over the passages over weeks. It was tremendously helpful, and I enjoyed it very much.

Some of the sermons in this book are from those chapel Sundays. Others are from Sunday morning worship in the sanctuary and some are from special occasions like Christmas Eve, a baptism, a Holy Week service.

The creativity, the intellectual work, and the inspiration of the Holy Spirit all combined for me in a marvelous and weighty, yet light and sparkling way for me to be a channel of God's word on a given Sunday. I thank God for giving me the opportunity and the challenge, the responsibility and the creative gifts to bring these matters to life. I hope you will find these sermons of use to you in your spiritual life despite the fact that they were written prior to the turn of the 21st century. None were written on a typewriter, however – all had the benefit of a computer!

Cheryl Gosa
Atlanta, GA
Winter 2019

The Fire and The Knife
Genesis 22:1-14; Psalm 13

"The fire and the wood are here, but where is the lamb for a burnt offering?"

Most of the time when we hear this Old Testament story, we know we are about to hear a sermon about the incredible willingness of a father to sacrifice his beloved and long-awaited son. We expect that it will be a sermon about faith and testing. Preachers dwell on the agony, the dread, the stoic obedience of Abraham and then revel in the nick-of-time salvation of Isaac with proof positive that Abraham is good enough and God is satisfied.

But today I want to look at this story from another direction. I want us to think about Isaac and his part in this story and in ours.

We are so used to hearing this story that the horror of it almost goes over our heads. We know how it comes out; we know Isaac is saved by a disembodied voice and the ram caught in the thicket. But the boy Isaac doesn't know how it will come out as it is happening to him. His father has asked him to go on a journey. We don't know his age, but the Bible refers to him as a boy which under Jewish law would certainly make him under the age of thirteen. Trustingly he trots along the path and it finally dawns on him that the fire and the knife are there, and they're headed for a mountain of sacrifice but where is the sacrificial animal? His father says the Lord will provide so Isaac walks on, trusting.

What then must Isaac have thought when his father stopped and set down his things and began to tie Isaac up?

What must Isaac have thought when his father picked him up and - put him on the altar stone?

The Bible doesn't report these details at all. The Bible is so focused on Abraham's obedience that Isaac's terror and confusion are lost in the pages of time.

Did he lie there docile like a stereotypical Bible character or did he cry out and struggle against his destiny?

What must Isaac have thought when his father's arm went high into the air with the shining knife reflecting the morning sun?

If you have children, you know how far a child's trust goes. In their younger years it is unquestioning. The father and the mother are like God and the child has no choice in, and in fact, no problem with trusting them completely.

But children have a limited perspective. Grownups at least have more direct experience in years. And yet when it comes to suffering and hard times and struggles we are all like little children with tunnel vision before God and we don't understand why it is happening to us and we wonder constantly when it will stop and what did we do wrong to cause it and how can we survive and what is on the other side of this hardship and unhappiness and despair and grief?

And either we cry out and struggle against God and life or we lie down and are tempted to just accept our fate as victims with stoicism and stone faces. But in either case when we have our feet to the fire and the knife is rising above our heads, we want to know the meaning of such an intense time in our lives.

Well, the first thing this story has to say to us has to do with trust.

The second thing has to do with the paradox of hope in believing that eventually there will be some way where there appears to be no way.

And the third thing we can take away from the story of Isaac on Mt. Moriah has to do with patience.

I

When we **trust** we are putting our lives into the hands of another, believing that that other is wiser at this moment than we are. As we go through life, it is repeated power exercised with a benevolent aim that enables us to believe that a more powerful one than we are can reliably have our best interests at heart.

If as children we had parents or surrogate parents who loved us and looked out for us, then when we are older, we can look back and remember those times and then we can put ourselves into the hands of something or someone and believe that they will be on our side.

And by extension then, we can trust God, the one we cannot see but come to believe in through faith. We can trust, in that case, even as we go through what is totally unknown to us or what feels like painful injustice. But even when we do have memories of that good kind of experience of trust it is so hard to remember it and relax into it when the tide has turned against us and shows no signs of ebbing.

Abraham was able to look back and see that God had indeed always been there for him. God had told Abraham and Sarah to pack up and move into the unknown, and trusting, they had done so. God had told Abraham and his wife long ago that they would have a child long after they were too old. And God had come through.

And now with this child of promise growing and learning and the love growing deeper and deeper with each passing day, Abraham's willingness to climb that mountain with his only son was built on a firm foundation of trust in God that his son Isaac had surely begun to hear about but had yet to experience in his own life.

And yet we know that Isaac was destined for great things. We know there's no way he could have been killed on that mountain because then we couldn't have had Jacob and Joseph and David and Jesus who came after him. We know that, yes, but Isaac was walking up a mountain without a clue as to what lay ahead. And when he saw the significance of the missing sacrificial animal and saw the knife and felt the fire and the ropes binding him, he had nothing to go on but the look in his father's eyes.

It must have happened very quickly. When those elemental

and sacred times happen, they pass as swiftly as the stroke of a knife through butter. There is no time to think, to reason, to ponder right action. There is likewise often no time to react, no time to feel the weight of the moment as it is happening. It is only later that we can ponder and find all kinds of other responses we could have made. Life happens too quickly sometimes for us to see it as it happens.

How many times in your life can you think of when you tried to fully live a moment as it happened because you knew it was a once-in-a-lifetime experience –

> the last instant before you said, "I do" and you would never again be just you alone,

> that last instant before the new baby cried for the first time and opened her eyes and looked at you and you were forever changed,

> the last instant before the casket lid was closed on that beloved face forever?

But as hard as you tried you just knew you weren't appreciating it enough. The next instant was pushing hard at the holy moment and then it was gone, living only in your memory and revisited at odd moments like ...

> waiting at a red light,

> in the middle of scrambling the eggs,

> in the still small hours of the night.

Philosophers call those fleeting, life-changing times at the top of the knife's arc - SYNCOPE - the pause before the motion goes the other way and life changes completely. An example is one of those clocks that has a series of little balls that go round and round for a few seconds, then they slow down, stop and begin to turn in the other direction. I'm always mesmerized by the turning balls when I see one of those clocks and hold my breath during the pause when they stop and then start up again in the other direction. That moment when they stop, before they start again is called SYNCOPE.

The Fire and the Knife

Remember the announcement of the O. J. verdict? Do you remember him standing there breathless as the jury foreman said "We find the defendant? ..... not guilty." That was a graphic pause of syncope for OJ and for us all. Or what about Juan Antonio Samaranch that September morning all those years ago "The 1996 Summer Olympic Games go to the city of .... Atlanta." Did you hold your breath, did you react? Our lives were never the same as residents of Atlanta after that pause of syncope in the life of a city.

Life is lived in a special way in those intense moments, those breathless pauses ...

> before the tide turns,
>
> before the music starts again,
>
> the suspended moment after we have breathed in and before we start to breath out again.

If we could open the doors,

> if we could widen out that time of syncope
>
> if we could make it last only a little longer,

I believe we would see the overall plan,

> we would understand our place in it,
>
> we would stand above the limited vision we have as human beings,
>
> we would know perfect trust and believe with perfect faith, for God stands in the syncope.

And yet we can only see God in brief flashes, for the light of God's countenance is too bright, the glory of God's being is too rich for human taste. And so, the flash of the sun on the knife's blade is as much as we can bear of divinity. That little pause is so short we can't really understand what happens there, we can only feel it with the soul and bring it into human understanding with the heart. We can only trust that it is there and know that it is part of an overall design that we will never come close to fully comprehending on this side of the veil of death.

But the Good News is that because God is a kind and loving God, because God created us in an image that reflects divinity, because God sent Jesus Christ to show us how to be truly and wholly human, we can trust that whatever is happening to us has meaning in the end.

"All things work together for good; all things work together for good" (Romans 8:28) we repeat like a mantra as we struggle through the devastating blows that life deals us. Isaac on the altar stone in that instant when the knife was ascending high into the air had to trust that there was meaning to this horrible thing that was happening to him at the hand of his own father.

Trust is a thing that is built on the past. In the depths of despair, we have only a shadowy vision of something called trust that carries us through. If we have even a glimmer of trust during pain, we can see it shining like a laser beam from far away and we can trust that we will survive.

The Good News is that we can trust God because of our past, and if not our personal past then the past that is revealed in Scripture and in the life of Jesus Christ. We can trust even what we cannot see, what we cannot even imagine and because we can trust we can also hope.

II

Hope is built on trust. Hope is that gentle and fragile feeling that refuses to believe that all is lost and that there is no reason to go on. Hope is aimed toward the future. We cannot hope if we don't believe in tomorrow. "This, too, shall pass, this, too, shall pass" is hope's popular mantra. If we didn't believe it then what would be the point of getting up in the morning? If what is happening now is all there is or ever will be then surely it would be better to go to sleep and never wake up.

The Fire and the Knife

When someone dear to us dies, it is trust that allows us to believe that God is grieving, too, for God grieved the loss of his own son, the best of all humanity. But it is hope that tells us that the pain will subside even if it will never fully go away.

We can hope at all because we believe that God is good, and that creation is good. If we didn't believe that then we would have no reason to go on.

I saw a film while I was up at Princeton one summer. It was a Dutch film shot in Belgium called "Antonia's Line." It was about community and acceptability and a village where eccentricity and strangeness were matter-of-factly woven into the fabric of life, where everyone had a place in the grand scheme of things. One man in the community was a brilliant philosopher, an atheist who in the end gave up on life for he had nothing to believe in. The rest of the community, despite the tragedies that befell them as the years went by, carried on with love and hope, believing in the power of togetherness and shared experience. Those who have a belief in God believe in the goodness of life. And those who believe in the basic goodness of creation have hope.

Hope is a fragile thing, like fiber optic cable.

Hope walks softly with kittens' paws and floats like a moth on the night air.

Hope is the lightning bug's little light glowing in a Mason jar in the vast summer backyard of our lives.

Hope calls to us in a voice we can barely hear, beckoning us on into a new day.

Hope is written all through the Bible in its visions of eternity. It threads through the stories from Genesis to Revelation as people of faith struggle to believe in a God always ahead of us, a God who became human and said follow me.

Hope is a gossamer feeling based on what can eventually

come to be if we only have patience.

III

Patience is a present concept. We can be patient right now, we can learn to wait for the right time, because we can trust the experience of the past and we can hope in a brighter future. But patience is a virtue that is in short supply in our time.

We don't need to be patient with a boring TV show for there are dozens of other programs on at this very moment and maybe something more interesting is going on over on channel 31 or channel 1031, for that matter!

We don't need to be patient on a hot summer night and slow our breathing down to cool ourselves off or lie awake and feel the oscillating fan go back and forth, back and forth, with that instant of syncope in the middle before it turns the other way, and wait for the coolness of the wee hours to bring relief. Air conditioning provides instant comfort, and cold drinks incessantly rumble out of vending machines.

And the process of life itself doesn't seem to require patience anymore. The long summers of our childhood tick-tocked slowly by in a haze of Kool Aid and Keds as we waited to grow up, all in good time. Time plodded along until we were sixteen and gained the freedom of wheels.

But today's children have less of an opportunity to learn the virtue of patience; they're too busy being delivered to the next activity on time, today, right now. But we are forced to be patient when our lives hit difficult times, and the rapid pace ceases to distract us as our hearts are affected.

When someone dies or when we have a long-term illness, or someone we love is slowly leaving us, all the manic schedules in the world don't make the time go by quickly enough and we are forced eventually to learn the patience of attending to time that we would rather avoid. When a loved one is suffering, we wish they would just let go, and then we feel guilty about that for we know that when they are gone, we will wish them back again for the rest of our lives. That kind of suffering on the cusp, the top of the knife's arc makes us afraid to fall either way and it takes enormous patience to live on that edge, to wait in that time of syncope for the right time, for God's time, for things to develop in order to know the next step to take.

And so, Isaac trusted his father for he had no choice. He certainly hoped that what looked like inevitable doom would not happen, and he lived out with patience the heart-stopping, suspended present of his very life as he lay on that smoldering altar and waited as the knife traveled up and poised at the top until the voice of God's angel rang out in the morning stillness.

The Old Testament commentators say that because God intervened on that mountain, because God had a bigger plan in mind, Isaac was given his life back again for a purpose, he was returned to life, he was resurrected. And it's not a giant leap to think about Jesus and what happened to him in the same terms.

IV

"Not my will, but yours be done," prayed our Lord in the garden, in abject wrenching **trust** of God. (Luke22:42)

"Today you will be with me in paradise," he proclaimed to the thief beside him as together they hung on **hope** alone. (Luke 23:43)

"Into your hands I commend my spirit," said Jesus (Luke 23:46) in the **patience** of syncope, the moment suspended between life and death, the instant before he fell over into the other realm, the moment of syncope between being Jesus and being no longer Jesus – the patience of the three days waiting, the syncope of suspended time between Good Friday and the new birth of Easter morning.

And because we are baptized into his death and resurrection, we, too, are given our lives back again each morning. The trust and hope and patience that sustained Jesus through his trials sustain us as well. Because Christ dwells within us we have "bread enough and to spare" (Luke 15:17) as we make our way through this human life. We sing these miracles every Sunday.

> *"If Thou but trust in God to guide thee,"*

> *"O God, our help in ages past, our hope for years to come"*

> *"Have Thine Own Way, Lord, Have Thine Own Way, While I Am Waiting"*

> *"There is a Place of Quiet Rest, Near to the Heart of God".*

These are the threads of our faith and we see them woven together in the parallel moments in time when Isaac lay vulnerable on a fiery altar and Jesus hung with piercing pain on a cruel cross. Their stories are our story, too, as heirs of the promise.

"The fire and the wood are here, my father," said Isaac, "but where is the sacrificial animal?" And his father replied, "the Lord will provide, my son." Isaac's question is our question.

> How is this to be?

> How am I to go on?

> How can this agony be of any use to anyone?

> When will it be over?

And Abraham's answer is the answer we hear in our heart of hearts. God answers through the moments of our lives, through the goodness of creation and the precious gift of life itself - "I will provide." With trust and hope and patience we live our days and nights and we catch glimpses of who God is in the blink-length moments of syncope when the windows of heaven open and shed bits of eternal light that are enough to propel us forward into another day.

On that first Easter morning the radiance of Jesus in the garden was the light of heaven.

The Fire and the Knife

The sun on Abraham's knife blade pierced Isaac's eyes as the voice of his salvation rang out with hope.

May the light of God's glory reach us in moments of despair and discouragement. giving us just enough trust and hope and patience to carry on until tomorrow.

In the name and in the marvelous light of Jesus Christ our Lord, Amen.

What Lies Ahead
Philippians 3:1-14

"But this one thing I do: forgetting what lies behind and straining forward to what lies ahead."

In his letter to the Philippians Paul shows himself to have a high regard for his readers and the book itself is one of the more joyous and upbeat of the letters attributed to Paul. But the apostle Paul is also one who is well known for saying exactly what he wants to say and for not pulling any punches.

Furthermore, when he is speaking passionately about his love for Jesus Christ and his commitment to following in the faith no matter what, he often shows that passion by the strong contrasts he draws with words. The passage this morning if it were translated literally contains slang and words we don't ordinarily say in church. For instance, King James renders Paul's word translated here "rubbish" as "dung". He uses such strong language about what to reject, as an equally vigorous parallel to the very strong prize and joy of knowing Jesus Christ. In other words, you can tell how strongly he feels about his subject by how strongly he speaks about the other side of the story.

The new Christians to whom Paul wrote had been through a great deal of turmoil and persecution in the early decades of the faith and Paul appears to feel the need here to jerk them out of their depression about that trouble. He also appears to be giving them a glorious pep talk about their true purpose and the goal of their striving. In short, he is trying to show them the intensity of the big picture as they struggle mightily along each step of the way.

When I was fifteen my father taught me to drive. It was in early fall that year in the middle 1960's and the weather was still warm since I was born in mid- September. After supper he'd drive us in our big old turquoise Chevrolet Impala to the cemetery in Dalton, Georgia where he'd ceremoniously stop the car, get out and trade places with me. After a basic lesson about which pedal controlled what, how to work the blinkers and the wipers, or the purpose of the emergency brake, I'd tool around the winding gravel roads where it was impossible to drive more than 10 miles per hour. I remember him sitting on the passenger side resting his elbow on the open window ledge, dangling a cigarette out the window as I drove sedately along. And I remember him over and over saying to me "look on down the road, Cheryl. You can't drive by looking at the little patch right in front of the car. You have to look on down the road." That was scary to me because I was terrified of what I was about to run over just beyond the hood of the car much less on down the road. But eventually I found that by looking out ahead I was able to steer more smoothly and to anticipate major obstacles like dogs and trash cans and the occasional overturned flower urn. By the time I advanced to driving out on the street I at least knew how to look ahead and was able to see cars coming down side streets and see stop signs before they were right in my face.

Paul urges his readers in Philippi to focus on what lies ahead. The martyrdom their colleagues was facing was ongoing and the grief must have been immense. But those who had died had gone on to God. What had happened was nothing compared to what lay ahead. Paul uses sports analogies often in his letters because he lived in a culture saturated by Rome and Greece, both of whom prized athletics. The game, winning the game, reaching the goal first, competition - all were important ideals. And we are not exempt. Our speech is full of baseball and football not to mention military references. Every day in the newspaper the Braves, win or lose, claim to have their minds on nothing but the next game. Forget the loss last night, the win today isn't too important either; the important thing is the next game and the rest of the season and the series.

When we drag the past along with us like so much baggage, we are hindered from running at all. When our tunnel vision is locked onto what happened to us last year or last week or even fifty years ago; when we wrap ourselves in the hurts and slights, we have sustained through the years like hair shirts, we can't move ahead, and we lose sight of the joy and the love that propels us through life in Christ. Though he wasn't making quite the same point, Marley's ghost covered in chains in Dickens' "Christmas Carol" is the image that comes to mind.

I think that's the point of forgiveness, too. Forgiveness happens in our hearts and is largely unaffected by what somebody else does or says. Regardless of whether someone says to us that they're sorry, we can either believe them or not, but we can't compel them to do anything more. We must make the change on the inside and move on.

Another reason to forget what lies behind and to look ahead is that the memories from the past will haunt us and color our lives from now on if we are unable to look on down the road and pray for faith to make it to better days. Bad things happen to good people all the time and the Psalms are full of thoughts about good things always happening to bad people. But I think Paul would admonish us not to worry about the good fortune of bad people or to dwell on our mistakes. Ours is to ask forgiveness from God, from others, from ourselves, and then to keep moving, keep believing and keep our eyes on the life which is ours solely by grace in Jesus Christ.

This is not to say that we must ignore hurt or pain or grief. Repressed feeling is something that will come back eventually and force us to deal with it. But we can feel it and acknowledge it and deal with it and move on, having made it a part of who we are, one of the scars we carry like chicken pox dents or small pox vaccination scars or bicycle wreck badges of courage. Our lives are maps of where we have been and who we have become.

Paul acknowledges that he has not reached the goal or obtained the final prize, but it is enough for him that he is on the way, that he is pressing on in the life that is laid out before him in Christ. My father's direction about the big picture rather than the little piece of road in front of the car is a way of urging me to keep perspective, that what is happening to us now is not how it will always be, that in the overall scheme of things the present struggle is only part of the story. All of us face this paradox of needing to see more broadly in order to stay steadily on the little piece of road which it has been given to us to walk.

On World Communion Sunday the church is the great meeting place of all of those who are trying to live every day, letting go of what was and greeting with open arms what the new day will

The Fire and the Knife

bring. It is a place of forgiveness, a place to leave behind the burdens of the past and the worries of the present. The future is ahead of us, but our little cars are on the road here and now in this place, 'Today, all around the world, Christians are joined at this table in common acknowledgement of our weakness, our strength, our humanity, our mistakes, our struggles and our glory as children of God. We find hope and love and faith for tomorrow. Together we understand the gain of knowing Christ which offsets, hands down, the struggle of the present or the past. And that gain gives us courage enough to face what lies ahead. Thanks be to God. Amen.

Garlands and Jewels
Isaiah 61:1-4, 8-11; I Thess. 5:16-24

"As a bridegroom decks himself with a garland, and as a bride adorns herself with her jewels."

The images in today's texts remind me so much of Christmas. The fact that they are the lectionary texts for today, the 3rd Sunday of Advent, always make me appreciate how the lectionary works so well and why I use it when I preach. Images of garlands and jewels just reek of Christmas trees, and the notion of robes and the anticipation of shoots springing up anew from the earth before too many weeks goes by fills me with joy.

The Isaiah text is a classic one, of course, in understanding Jesus' mission on earth and in our understanding of what a Messiah is supposed to do. But for me, it is also a passage filled with God's love for us as the people God created and for the earth on which we live.

The passage from Thessalonians continues the theme of joy and love and acts as a counterpoint to the Old Testament prophecy. For by the time of the New Testament text the deed which Isaiah foretold had happened, the Messiah had come, and we now live in the light of his coming. The writer of the letter to the Thessalonians writes to his readers clothed by virtue of their baptism into Jesus Christ, in the very jeweled robe and garland that Isaiah talked about.

And then the end of the Thessalonians passage points us in a circle to what we await in just a couple of short weeks. "May your spirit be kept sound at the coming of our Lord Jesus Christ."

For it is in Advent that

we are captured by the paradox of remembering something that happened long ago

anticipating its commemoration in our very human time, very shortly indeed and then anticipating in a less comprehensible way the return of Christ eventually.

And at Communion we celebrate all three of those aspects of time every time we eat this bread and drink this cup. We remember what happened in an upper room. We commune with that same Savior this day, and we understand this meal to be a foretaste of a festal banquet which is yet to come.

This paradox of time, this holding of the tension of many things being symbolized in one act, is our burden and our joy as human beings. We live an existence governed by the ticking of a clock counting the seconds of our lives and the life of the world, but our minds and spirits are capable of transcending that limited notion of time to hold the slippery tension of timelessness, what we call eternity.

Kathleen Raine is a British poet well into her 90's who is revered in her country as "the major living poet of the English language." She is in the habit of writing a poem to include with her Christmas cards each year and her poem for 1989 speaks to this idea of time in a way that I want us to think about as something we can grasp and perhaps then begin to understand exactly what the birth and life of one man two thousand years ago has to do with my life and yours today. Listen for some wise words indeed:

"As this year yet again, the days draw in
Toward the dark solstice and the holy birth
I open my old address book, and the new,
Go through the many names once written down
To be remembered, some already forgotten.
Every year, for the duration of the timeless moment
It takes to write a message on a card,
Address an envelope, I am with that friend again:
'With love', I write, as through the alphabet a name
For a moment holds my thought, as once
We were present to one another wholly, each to each,
Here and now, for an hour, for a day,
A month, a year, in some familiar place,
Dim, half-forgotten now, once home,

College rooms, a shared table, a shared task -
a friend, to whom for a moment or a day
I was wholly present once, as you to me,
Did we not bring to that moment of meeting?
Each a whole life
As we passed one another in the great kaleidoscope?
'With love', I write to each, to each my whole love,
For love is indivisible, infinite,
Though we, who think to give
All to one or few among the many presences
Of the one presence, are slow to learn
That every face is a face of the one beloved.
Two hundred, more or less, I have remembered
Among those who have come and gone, to me and from me,
As I to them, and with a pang
I write on another card, 'With love from",
And sign my name, which, it may be,
They too will remember with the love
That brings together and parts, over and over
Our many-in-one, who would be infinitely
With each other always, were it not for time."

    Kathleen Raine has hit upon the secret of life, to my mind. And that secret is called love. There is a vast sea of it, infinite, and out of that love was born the human race and the earth. Out of that vast sea of love came Jesus as the face of God. And the love of Jesus Christ for each of us is as infinite as the vast sea from which he, too, drew. And because there is such a vastness to that sea of love, and because that sea is one sea, the sea we touch today is the same sea that Jesus himself touched. When we break this bread and drink this cup, we are joined through the miracle of timelessness with the love of one man who was born to show us how to be fully human. He loved us, we love him and though our human lives are separated by so many years we are present to each other and to him in this sacrament. Our spirits and souls are timeless and transcend the limitations of human life. The love we feel for him is felt by him as surely as we taste the bread and the cup.

    Were it not for time we would all be together always. The Good News is that the love we shared with those friends and family who are away from us now is still part of the vast sea of love that is God and which we touch through the life of Jesus of Nazareth. And our lives are connected to the life of Jesus Christ whose birth we celebrate and whose life we anticipate being born anew in us over and over in our own lives.

We are part of that love which created us, which chooses for us garlands and jewels instead of ashes and sorrow. Peace and rejoicing, thanksgiving and prayer fill our lives. The writer tells us "do not quench the Spirit" for in keeping the flow open to the Spirit's power, we keep the door wide to touch and taste the love that forms our lives.

Thanks be to God for the coming of Christ repeatedly throughout time and eternity.

One Fine Day
Isaiah 25:6-10

"On this mountain the Lord of hosts will make for all peoples a feast of rich food, a feast of well-aged wines, of rich food filled with marrow, of well-aged wines strained clear."

Last week I heard on National Public Radio about the 13-year-old boy in Chicago who was pulled from his bike and beaten severely. He's comatose in the hospital and his attackers are boys 17, 18 and 19 years old. The 13-year-old is black, the attackers are white. You probably read about it yourself.

Here we are 2 days after Easter, that most glorious day of the Christian year when jubilation and alleluias are the order of the day and yet we sigh even during the celebration, knowing it won't last, not if we're human.

The boys in Chicago who have been arrested for the attack are parochial school students and as I rode along listening to the news my mind made an immediate leap of anger and puzzlement as to why that school did not do a better job of teaching those boys about love of neighbor and the meaning of Easter. Then I thought a little more deeply about a man I know, a product of the Polish Catholic mean streets of Chicago, who would never in a million years attack a thirteen-year-old boy on his bicycle but I've heard him say things that were the verbal equivalent of fists and hardnosed boots striking somebody whose only crime is being different, maybe in the wrong place at the wrong time.

And I thought about all of us here, leaders in a church which preaches the never- ending grace and steadfast love of God shown to us in Jesus Christ and living within us as Holy Spirit, And I thought about Sunday School classes and children learning Bible stories and the Ten Commandments and about respecting others and self and God. And I wondered as I have before if it will be enough. And I thought maybe we just must do the best we can to teach our children the right way to be and then hope they'll be OK.

The Fire and the Knife

A man in our church stopped me in the parking lot last Sunday and said "I want to ask you a question. You're a spiritual person and well versed in these matters. Why was my car involved in a collision last week when I had summoned all God's angels to surround my car and protect me from crashes? Why did that happen? What went wrong? I asked for protection and it didn't work." I said "I don't know the answer to your question. Sometimes things just happen. Maybe a little chink in the protective armor." A lame answer but all I could come up with on the spot with my child standing by all ears for she believes completely in angels and their guardian function.

From angels to vicious attackers. How are we to live in these times? Will it ever end? Will it ever even get better? What's the use of Easter anyway if we must keep hearing about everything from crime against persons to the mystery of guardian angels sleeping at the wheel?

Well, that's why God gave us Isaiah 25, I think. In a cynical mood I guess we could call it a carrot dangling always just ahead of us that we'll never reach but in the spirit of Easter I propose that we see it positively as evidence that all will be well one fine day and that we must live today as if it were already that fine day.

The ultimate fine day will take place on a mountain and the feast there will be the finest you've ever seen - all your favorite foods. I always joke that if I go to hell, all there'll be to eat is egg whites, anchovies and tomato aspic. But if you happen to like those foods, your hell will contain a different menu. On the other hand, if I make it to heaven, to that magic mountain of Isaiah 25, the table will be spread with boiled peanuts, fried okra, smoked oysters, Johnny cakes, real mashed potatoes and perfect peaches. What will the banquet table hold for you on that fine day?

And on that mountain God will have destroyed the shroud of fear and cynicism and apathy that is spread over this world this week and next week not to mention last week. God has swallowed up death forever, of course. That is what we celebrated Sunday.

And God will wipe away our tears. It doesn't say in this

passage that there will be no more tears, but that God will be with us to hold us and dry the tears. That's hopeful. And we will all stand on that mountain saying this is our God, the one we have waited for; we will rejoice and be glad. For God's hand will rest on that mountain.

To make it to the top of that mountain is a matter of time and patience. We can't gauge the height of the mountain or how long it will take to get there as we climb, but I believe we will see

> wrecked cars whose angels have been derelict in their duty
>
> and here and there will be boys on bicycles who don't make it home.
>
> And there will be damaged children in grownup bodies spewing hate
>
> and there will be women not knowing their power and men who know theirs all too well.

And we know that we can't just keep walking resolute in our purpose ignoring these tragedies strewn along the path. It is ours

> to right the bicycle
>
> to lend a hand to the women and to the damaged men
>
> to pick up the child and carry her a while
>
> to stop a squabble over a bit of bread
>
> to speak up for the one being ridiculed.

But at the top of the mountain, we must believe, will be laid a feast the likes of which we cannot know. Our only clue, our only taste is that which we receive in our hearts and among our brothers and sisters in Christ as we share the moments, the open windows of worship and fellowship that cause us to glimpse the feast just for a moment.

The Fire and the Knife

In the Lord's Supper, in the moments of worship where God causes us to have hope, in the moments when we open ourselves to receive the faith that is a gift, and which sustains us for the climb - we can find courage to keep walking. This is Easter time and for fifty days we are instructed to walk with joy, before Pentecost and its extra burst of love descends upon us, After Pentecost the windows will close, and we will walk again, as Greek Orthodox scholar Alexander Schnemann puts it, "in the night of time and history, of the daily effort, of the fatigue and temptations, of the whole inescapable burden of life". The Good News though is that we carry that burden knowing that one fine day we'll make it to the top of the mountain and find their everlasting joy.

Thanks be to God!

The Unexpected Life
John 3:1-9

"The wind blows where it chooses, and you hear the sound of it, but you do not know where it comes from or where it goes."

It's easy to miss the point of what Jesus must tell us in this story of Nicodemus and his wonder at being born again. We quickly get sidetracked onto the dual teaching about being born first of the water of baptism and then somehow also getting the Holy Spirit. Or more concretely, we can follow that we are born of water at our actual physical birth and are willing to accept that somewhere along the way we also get an infusion of the intangible Holy Spirit which makes us "real" Christians. But I think Jesus is going deeper, he is being more paradoxical than that. John is the gospel writer who is the master of symbolism and metaphor. He loves the poetry of language and the hidden ambiguities of spiritual matters. Nothing is as it seems upon first reading.

Here comes Nicodemus, a Pharisee, a stickler for details, a rational man, one devoted to logic, to decency and order who is trying to understand who this man Jesus is. He begins by faith granting that he knows Jesus is a man of God because it follows that a person who does such wondrous signs as miracles must be in God's presence in a special way. But Jesus quickly confounds his logic with an enigmatic saying about not being able to see anything without being born from above.

Nicodemus tries again. His brain simply will not let him relinquish logic. He follows Jesus' tack and asks how anybody can be born twice since everybody knows it's a one-way street out of the womb. Jesus again replies by bringing up spirit and going on about the wind. Finally, Nicodemus gives up and in wonder and bewilderment asks, "How can this be?"

And that is our question, too. Over and over we wonder how can this be? How can our lives be the way they are? How can the world be the way it is? If we could only understand, maybe we could accept. If we could only organize and categorize properly, then maybe we could be at peace.

At a conference last week, I was in a small group of interesting people who met every day to discuss the presentations we had been hearing. My group consisted of a Jungian therapist, a businesswoman, an artist, a psychotherapist of the behavioral persuasion, and a retired research physicist. Somehow, we got off on quantum physics and the new scientific thinking about how the world works and how everything is interconnected and how the scientists are turning out to be theologians after all. The physicist tried to explain to us how the meteorologists were learning to predict hurricanes by applying force field theory and how certain force fields produced certain weather patterns which made a hurricane go up this street instead of down that street.

Well, then the behavioral guy got all excited about how everything could be so neatly categorized and organized and wasn't that marvelous our growing ability to know exactly where a hurricane was going to strike, down to the exact street. The artist looked at him and said "well, it is pretty amazing, I guess, but all the time those people are working so hard to figure it out, the hurricane is blowing wherever it wants to anyway and there's nothing they can do about it even if they do know why it's going where it's going".

Hurricanes, my friends, are not the only things that go where they want to go no matter what we figure out and rationalize about them. All the understanding in the world, all the explanations in the world don't stop life from happening to us when we least expect it. While we're busily trying to organize tomorrow, today hits us in the face. But surely there is no comfort in just letting life happen when we are 21st century American citizens, not when we have technology and science well in hand, when we have computers and digital watches and cars and planes that go and fly with mathematical precision. We are trained to trust the body of accumulated knowledge of these centuries that have made our country what it is.

But Nicodemus was also relying on a body of knowledge which had held his people together for centuries, the knowledge in God's holy written word which showed them how to live, down to the words and actions of dawn and of sunset. All could be mastered if all could be understood and ritually followed.

And here comes Jesus saying you don't have any idea what will happen anyway even if you have it all figured out. And if you can just believe that God can be trusted with your life, then you can fear and marvel at the power of hurricanes without having to understand how they work. You can respect the awesome majesty of that wind and rain and respond to it accordingly. Can't you just see the scientists frantically working their equations and tapping on their computers predicting where the hurricane will go and just as they figure it out and jump up in horror, the doors and windows burst open and wind and rain sweep them all away for in fact, the hurricane was coming right down their street. Didn't do them much good to know how and why in the end.

To be born of the Spirit is to know that the wind blows where it will, that the wind comes and goes without our being able to see it. But we can see it, that elusive power of the Spirit, if we will only admit it into our lives and trust it. If we can let it blow through our logical days and our rational nights, our organized weeks and clockwork years then we can clearly and truly see that Jesus was a man in the presence of God and because he died and rose again and sent the Holy Spirit to dwell within us, we, too, are people in the presence of God.

We will know it by the signs that cross the centuries from his time to ours. We can see the signs in the way the wind blows through our own lives and the life of the world, bringing new life and hope, and creativity and imagination and love in unexpected illogical, irrational ways. If we are open to seeing it.

God is with us and within us. God is right here. Someone said God is like humidity. You can't see it, but you can feel it as sure as the world, especially in Georgia in the summertime. This table before us is like the wind of the Spirit. We can't see how Jesus Christ is present to us in this bread and in this cup. But we can feel it as we eat and drink, the wind of the Spirit blowing through and through us, washing us clean and sweeping away whatever is separating us like a veil of smog from the presence of God and each other. We are the Body of Christ in this place and we know it in a way that the meteorologists can never explain.

"How can these things be?" we ask but the answer is not something we can see on a screen or read in a book. It is something we know, something we feel, like a breeze in an otherwise still room - like this one. Thanks be to God for the unexpected life which we have received through Christ Jesus our Lord. Amen.

The Last Laugh
Mark 5:21-43

"Why do you make a commotion and weep? The child is not dead but sleeping." And they laughed at him.

Today's story is a familiar one. It's one of those stories with a subplot that parallels the main story. Sometimes we hear the story of the woman with the hemorrhage and sometimes we hear about Jairus' daughter but the writer has put them together to show us how both deal with healing. One of a girl who is almost a woman, the other was a grown woman in the throes of that middle phase of a woman's life.

But today I want to focus on the very end of the story. Jesus said to them "why are you weeping? She's not dead, she's sleeping. And they laughed at him." They laughed at him.

From our perspective it sounds almost sacrilegious, doesn't it? The very idea of laughing at Jesus takes our breath today. Our mothers told us we would be struck dead by lightning for that kind of disrespect of God.

But to the people gathered round that day wasn't he just a guy who was going around doing outrageous things and saying things that were blasphemous? He consorted with crazy people and was the fellow they knew as the son of Joseph the carpenter and here he is saying the girl isn't dead when everybody could see that she was.

But then again, so far, as Mark tells it,

Jesus has cast out an unclean spirit

healed lots of people at Simon's house

cleansed a leper, a paralytic, a man with a withered hand, and the Gerasene demoniac and then to top it off, has stilled a storm. The man is on a roll and we're only in chapter 5!

Matthew reports this same double story including the laughter and so does Luke. It must be an important lesson if we must hear it three times to begin to get it, whatever the point is.

The other famous incident of laughter in the Bible is, of course, the one about Abraham and Sarah having a baby when they are both hovering around 100 years old. The Bible says Abraham got such a kick out of the idea that he fell on the ground laughing. Sarah was more discrete, chuckling behind the tent flap.

And there is a report of a story later in Genesis when the Jewish leader Judah instructs his guards to back off after an incident, otherwise they'll be laughed at.

Ridicule and scorn are not welcome. To be laughed at is demeaning and humiliating and embarrassing and it causes one to think less of herself and her abilities, by its very nature. There's a superiority that comes across from the laughers that puts the laughee in his place.

On the other hand, Ecclesiastes tells us that there is a time to laugh just as there is a time to weep. So, there is good laughter and bad laughter. Indeed, after Isaac is born, Sarah proclaims that "God has brought laughter to me, and all who hear will laugh with me". (Gen 21:6) That's the good kind of laughter.

There is the laughter that mingles with shouts of joy. There is the laughter of remembering good times together. There is the laughter of love that delights in a child's mishandling of the English language. And yet the child might hear the laughter the other way and feel diminished.

That's one of the trickiest parts of growing up, learning to discern when you are being laughed at in the ominous and sad way, and being laughed with in the way of love and joy. And it is so crushing to think you are being laughed with when in fact you are being laughed at.

Recently I saw the movie *Emma*. There is the clever Emma who tries to direct everybody's life and she is so charming she tends to get away with it. Then there is Miss Bates, who is obnoxiously and blatantly verbose; she chatters on and on and on never knowing how grating she is on the group.

At a picnic, in the repartee of the moment, the group is playing a game where everybody can make three comments about a given subject and the chatterer says, why, that's her favorite subject. Emma says no doubt, but you're only allowed three comments and basically the game will be to see if you can do it.

Everybody laughs including the hapless Miss Bates but slowly she gets it as everybody freezes, knowing Emma has overstepped her bounds and turned friendship into cruelty. Miss Bates is humiliated by Emma's laughter of derision and doubt and realizes that all this time she has been merely tolerated and barely at that.

We automatically read today's story with that bad kind of laughing in mind. They laughed in derision and doubt at Jesus when he said the little girl was not dead.

But do you think it might be possible that their laughter might have included some of the other kind of laughter, that they were laughing from the other perspective, out of a pent-up excitement and hope that he would do it again this day, that there might be another miracle and they were going to be there to see it?

One of Job's friends tells him that "God will yet fill your mouth with laughter and your lips with shouts of joy". (Job 8:21) Is it possible that the laughter at Jairus' house included the laughter of anticipation,

> that spirit we get into just before the fireworks start
>
> that feeling of wonder at what is about to come
>
> that joy that bubbles up in laughter?

The writer of Ecclesiastes also says that "feasts are made for laughter and wine gladdens life". (Ecclesiastes 10:19) The table before us is one that anticipates the day when all together, we will feast at the king's table. At the end of time, when Jesus comes, we will be together in the heavenly banquet, feasting and laughing.

Our tradition has stressed the solemnity of this table relating it most often to the sacrifice of Jesus and to our own penitential unworthiness to partake. But the other tradition that we have lost but which is every bit as valid and which must be held in tension with the solemn feeling, is that this table is a joyful feast that is a foretaste of glory.

We come to the table in anticipation of being with Jesus Christ forever, surrounded by friends and fellow feasters, knowing that the joy we feel is the love that wells up in hope of and in thanksgiving for the grace that continues to be poured out in our lives.

These are the gifts of God for the people of God. And we can be joyful and thankful that God will have the last laugh and will lead the merriment when we are together at last for eternity. Thanks be to God for the unspeakable riches of glory that come to us in shouts of laughter! Amen.

Full Moon over Managua
Ephesians 2:11-22

"So then you are no longer strangers and aliens, but you are citizens with the saints and also members of the household of God."

Some people collect seashells or postage stamps or coins. Some people collect antique cars or depression glass or Barbie dolls. Some people collect baseball cards or those painted china plates that are advertised in the slick pages of the Sunday paper. I happen to collect video footage of the full moon all over the world. I have a particularly stunning view of the full moon over Port-au-Prince, Haiti taken from the balcony of the Hotel Montana looking out toward the bay. The Hotel Montana is gone now due to a hurricane but I still have the footage. I also have the full moon on a clear winter's night in London. Then there's the spectacular one over the ancient Christian Abbey in Scotland on the island of Iona. I would have had full moon over Kinshasa, Zaire, too, except there was no portable video in 1976 when I was there.

But my best shot by far is the full moon over Managua, Nicaragua with the clouds racing across it. How many of you have ever been to Managua? Raise your hand. Not many. Managua is not exactly a Delta Dream Vacation destination. Not an "in" place at all.

The first time I went to Nicaragua, there was a revolution going on and if you were sympathetic to the revolution you were sure that there was a contra with an American funded rifle behind every bush. If you were against the revolution you were sure there was a Communist plot in every speech by President Daniel Ortega. There was hostility in the air. There were black and red flags flying everywhere and up in the mountains there was fear. I felt it even before the American social worker was killed mere miles from where we slept in a mountain lodge.

The second and third times I went to Managua, it was in the aftermath of the long battle for control of that little country which had been abandoned in the end as the drama of world politics moved on to another global hot spot. I was there those two times to produce videos about a relief effort of manufacturing and fitting artificial arms and legs for wounded soldiers on both sides of the conflict. And it was on one of those nights after shooting emotional footage all day long that I looked up and saw the full moon with clouds scudding across it. And I added it to my collection.

Now the ironic thing about this hobby, of course, is that I'm the only one that knows one full moon from another. For you see I just turn on the camera and point up at the sky and there it is. I know exactly which one is which. But if you were to see the footage, you'd not know if it was Full Moon Over Timbuktu or Cape Town, Buenos Aires or Zurich.

The even funnier thing about my hobby, of course, is that there's no such thing as one full moon over Managua and a different full moon over Port-au-Prince. It is, in fact, the very same moon. When you're looking up at it though, wherever you are in the world, your heart thinks it's the full moon of that place, even though your mind says, of course, there's only one moon. Remember that old song, "I see the moon, the moon sees me, under the shade of the old oak tree, please let the moon that shines on me, shine on the one I love." Well, of course the same moon is going to shine on the one I love, It's the same moon.

On the other side is that song from the children's movie about the mouse that gets lost from its mother. In that song the lyricist understands it's the same moon and that's comforting "somewhere out there beneath the pale moon light, some one's thinking of me and loving me tonight." You look up at the moon and it is possible to feel the connection with all those who are at that moment also looking up at the same moon.

Another thought - did you ever imagine that on the other side of the night sky is a lot of light that is heaven and the stars are tiny glimpses of that other bright side? The moon, then, would be just a big hole through which to see heaven. And once a month we get a good look when the moon is full.

Or take the metaphor to another level. A baby is about to be born and suddenly a light, like the full moon, begins to shine and the baby moves toward it, carried along by an irresistible force. It is terrifying but there is life on the other side. The same could be said of death. Is it like emerging from a womb to be born into the light of something totally unimaginable?

Being citizens of this fragile earth, our island home, with its views of the full moon over whatever city in which we find ourselves. is like living inside a Faberge egg and looking out of the pinhole that is left when the egg was made. And when we die, we'll be able to see the light that surrounds the egg and the delicate and intricate tracery and colors that decorate the outside of the egg. And on this fragile earth, we sit in the United States of America, in the southern part, by the grace of God, in the great state of Georgia, in the fair city of Atlanta, in Midtown on the corner of 16th and Peachtree in a sanctuary, in our separate pews. beside our family members and our friends, inside our own bodies. Each reflecting the spirit of God and looking for the face of Christ with every step we take. Each of us looking out of our own souls into the light of the world. Each of us feeling separate and alone- outsiders in one way or another.

Well, what does this image of the moon have to do with Ephesians 2? It has to do with the fact that God's temple, the dwelling place of God, is one place but also many places depending on how you look at it or for it. And what makes up God's dwelling place is not just one thing or one place or even one person but again, it depends on how you look at it. Like looking at the moon, it's a matter of perspective which requires a willingness to live with the paradox, the tension, the ambiguity of life with God and life on this earth.

The paradox lies in our individual feelings of being outsiders during all this unity which sounds so good on paper. The letter to the Ephesians is emphatically anti-faction. It stresses unity. We are one Family, we are one Body, we are one City, one Household, one Temple, one dwelling place for God. And that edifice is built around Jesus Christ, the cornerstone.

The indisputable thread that weaves its way throughout the Bible is that God's dwelling place is among us and God will go with us and will not forsake us and whenever we want to be with God we have only to look within and around us and God is there. Wherever we are in the world, we are transformed by being in God's presence.

And this is the important part - because we are a people with a genetic unity as residents of this planet, that unity makes us strong enough to live lives of obedience and compassion for others and gives us the strength not to be afraid of anybody else and what they might represent to us. For our strength is ultimately in the one who is strong enough to lead us into new places, new forms of being, new shapes like the moon as it waxes and wanes. We can trust the God who holds us together even if we don't know or can't understand everybody else and their point of view.

We can feel alone at the same time we feel united. It isn't one or the other and it doesn't have to be. The moon can be one moon and it can also poetically feel like the moon over Managua and the moon over Atlanta. The one thing that doesn't change and that is a paradox is that God, like the moon, is with us.

The writer to the Ephesians uses three specific metaphors to talk about where God dwells and how it works to be a united people living in mutual support and respect despite our feelings of being separate and alone.

I

The first metaphor is of a city and the writer talks about the people who live in that city. We are not strangers and aliens, says verse 19 of our text. The Greek word that is used for strangers in verse 19 is a word that means "outsiders." This is not merely a person who is passing through, a traveler. This Greek word speaks of those who live beside everybody else, those who are tolerated, incidental to the bigger group and nothing more. These are the people that Christians are not, according to Ephesians. Baptized people are not merely tolerated outsiders, baptized people are full citizens with all the rights of those who live in the city of God. And there are no second-class citizens in God's city. Even the people who on the surface appear to be unacceptable to the collective, who don't fit in somehow, are nevertheless indispensable to the effort.

The Fire and the Knife

Do you remember Boo Radley in *To Kill a Mockingbird?* A shadowy figure if there ever was one. A misunderstood member of the community. An outsider who lived beside the others, who was fearfully tolerated but did not seem to participate in the life of the community. The Radley house was weird, nobody had ever been inside according the young Scout Finch who gives us this vivid description.

> "Rain-rotted shingles drooped over the eaves of their verandah; oak trees kept the sun away. Inside the house lived a malevolent phantom. People said he existed, but Jem and I had never seen him. People said he went out at night when the moon was dark and peeped in windows. When people's azaleas froze in a cold snap, it was because he had breathed on them A baseball hit into the Radley yard was a lost ball and no questions asked. The Radleys kept to themselves, a predilection unforgivable in Maycomb. Jem said Boo was about six-and-a-half feet tall. he dined on raw squirrels and any cats he could catch. There was a long-jagged scar that ran across his face, what teeth he had were yellow and rotten; his eyes popped, and he drooled most of the time."

At the end of the book, of course, Boo saves the children's lives from Bob Ewell's butcher knife in the park. The real Boo Radley, when Scout finally saw him, had a thin frame, a very white face, hollow cheeks, a wide mouth and gray eyes. He seemed nice to Scout, but then her father Atticus always said people were generally real nice when you finally see them.

II

The second metaphor the writer of Ephesians uses is that of a household. "We are members of the household of God" says verse 19. And that includes not only the proper children but also the ones referred to out loud or tacitly as the black sheep and the stepchildren and the illegitimate children. In God's house there are no children who are loved less than the others, there are no favorites, no one is in danger of being left out of the will. There are no children who receive special privileges or whose privileges are withheld as punishment. In the household of God, we are all equally children and heirs of the promise.

III

The third metaphor is of a building and we are each an indispensable part of that building. Some of you know that I am a volunteer gardener at Historic Oakland Cemetery. I don't have a yard, so this is my way of being grounded and working with dirt and flowers. The other day the cemetery keeper, Allen, was explaining to me why it is better for the walls around the burial plots to be made of bricks instead of slabs of granite. It seems that the slabs of granite are large and immovable, and it takes a team of men to even pick one up and place it and eventually when the dirt shifts and tree roots grow deep, the slab just gets pushed out of the way by the life it attempts to restrain, and it crashes down into a million pieces. On the other hand, the bricks are tied together, says Allen, using a masonry construction term, and they can give and there is room for the shifting matter within the walls.

Each person is separately a temple of the Holy Spirit but when joined to other temples each person becomes a living stone - a temple which is the Body of Christ, the Church. John Calvin said that when God dwells in each of us, it is God's will that we should embrace all in holy unity. He says in his "Institutes" that "around Christ, all the rest of the building is fitted together into a dedicated temple of the Lord. And you are all a vital part of God's Spiritual dwelling place."

The Good News of the gospel is that Jesus Christ is both the support for this dwelling place that is the Church and the mortar that enables it to grow and holds it together as it grows. It's like a glowing ball of material that can be shaped, reshaped, and molded into many things though the substance remains the same. It's like Play-Dough or Silly Putty. It is like the moon, waxing and waning from our perspective, shaped differently throughout the month but still always the same ball of material.

The Fire and the Knife

My daughter has a video game called Pandemonium. At the start of the game the character who runs the obstacle course that is the game, is a girl who literally glows. Those are her powers, I'm told, and she can lose them, and she can regain them. But as she moves along the path the glow goes with her and enables her to better overcome the challenges before her on each level of the game.

Each of us has that glow, those powers, like a pilot light in the furnace that we can't always see but which is always lit and ready to spring to even bigger life. That symbolic inner steady light is visible symbolically in the sky as the moon which reflects the light of the sun. The glow is there even during those three days of every month when the moon is dark. Like Christ in the tomb before Easter morning, there is darkness when the light appears to go out but then it returns and grows.

"Somewhere out there under and beyond the pale moonlight, someone's thinking of us and loving us tonight." Somebody human for just about everybody and somebody divine for all of us.

This world is full of quite tangible everyday people that God loves with an everlasting and steadfast love. These are people we are rationally sure must be outside God's all-loving embrace for one reason or another. Can you think of any today? These are people whom we unconsciously fear in the deepest places of our souls for one reason or another. And they are also the ones we know the best - ourselves - whom we fear in the deepest places of our souls to be somehow unacceptable. But each one of us is in progress, shifting and changing, growing and being shaped by Almighty God into the people God would have us be. Each one is tied to each other one.

All of us,

full of shame and doubt

full of anger and guilt

full of fear and righteous indignation

nevertheless, make up the glowing and infinitely strong Body of Christ. And that's the paradox - we are separate and full of fear and yet we are joined together into a body that is built of strength and confidence and love.

We look up at the moon and feel small, but we can also feel secure in the knowledge that there are millions and billions of other individuals who also look up at the moon and we are all together under the same moon.

But the most awesome thought of all to me is that this is the very same moon that Jesus Christ himself looked up and saw two thousand years ago. And the moon is still there, an enduring witness in the skies, a symbol that we can almost reach out and touch, that God loves us as a group and as individuals forever. We are inside God's love like babies in a womb, like fragile inhabitants of a Faberge egg, like indispensable parts of a body, a household, a building, the dwelling place of God.

This morning in Managua, Nicaragua the Christians throughout that city are gathered in little churches with brick walls and tin roofs under the hot sun, praising Jesus Christ and celebrating the presence of the Holy Spirit among them. They are celebrating the Lord's Supper with mismatched chipped little glasses and chunks of locally baked bread and they are singing and praying for you and for me. They are looking up at the moon and hoping for the best for their children, just like we do. Citizens, beloved children, living stones, we all form the dwelling place of God and the moon shines bright on every one of us equally, wherever we are and wherever we go in the world.

Thanks be to God for life, and for love and for grace poured out without measure. Amen.

Imitators of God
Ephesians 4:25-5:2

"Therefore, be imitators of God, as beloved children, and live in love, as Christ loved us and gave himself up for us, a fragrant offering and sacrifice to God."

Wow, that's a tall order. How in the world can we be expected to be imitators of God? Surely Paul is off on one of his ecstatic head trips. Even he didn't presume to be that high and mighty,

And he adds insult to injury when he says for us to live in love, the kind that Jesus displayed when he gave up his life for us. That's a little more down to earth but even so, it's way beyond what we can do. My Bible translation labels this passage "Rules for the New Life", Among the many rules included here are

- speak the truth

- be angry but do not sin

- do honest work and give to the needy

- let no evil talk come out of your mouth

- do not grieve the Holy Spirit (now there's a vague and ominous one)

- put away bitterness and wrangling and slander

- be kind to one another

A tall order any way you look at it. We can assume based on our experience of long years as part of the faith that God speaks the truth, is kind and doesn't get involved in bitterness and slander.

But it is curious that Paul tells us to imitate God. There are many references in the New Testament to being imitators of Christ but being called upon to imitate God is rarer. It's enough to make you want to sit very still believing that if you don't move you can't do anything wrong. Sort of like a frog in a gigger's light or a rabbit in the headlights.

"Be angry but don't sin" is, as a rule, too often lived out by repressing anger and having it eat away at you from the inside out.

"No bitterness, no wrangling, no slander, no evil talk, only honest work". This is a recipe for people who are seen but not heard.

"Speak the truth" is a bit daring for it can backfire and be heard as anger, bitterness, evil talk and slander. Not much assurance that it will be heard the way you intend. And, of course, "If you can't say anything nice about somebody, don't say anything at all" is the first ingrained commandment from your mother.

OK, so where does that leave us?

Give to the needy. Yes, we can do that.

Work hard, yes, we can do that.

Be kind, yes, we can do that.

Forgive people, yes, we can do that. Sometimes.

We can do all those things at fairly little risk to life and limb. And that is the first commandment of fatherly advice. "Keep your nose clean." But seen as a group, how can we live out these rules for the new life and by so doing, imitate God. Well, at the base of these exhortations is love.

We can't love as much as God or as completely as Jesus, but we can begin to love like that kind of love - a fragment of the eternal and overwhelming love that has been shown us. Like an atom against the picture of the universe we have been infused with the DNA of that kind of love for we are created in God's image and God is love. We can do no other.

But how? The sub-sentences for all these rules give us a host of clues about what it means to live this new life. Listen to a compilation of the second parts of the sentences that follow each imperative rule in this passage:

> We are members of one another,
>
> we need to say what will build up the body, so that our words may give grace to those who hear,
>
> we are marked with the Holy Spirit, so be tenderhearted for God in Christ has forgiven you,
>
> we are beloved children, so live in love, a fragrant offering to God.

Those sound pretty good when you separate them from the intimidating rules and commandments. In fact, it's like hearing a hammer pounding on the downbeat and hearing blessed silence on the upbeat. Do you hear the thumping musical rhythm of this passage? BOOM boom boom boom BOOM boom boom boom.

Now this is not to say that God is the heavy downbeat and we are the weaker upbeats. I think it's the reverse, that we find ourselves with the heavy downbeats, totally forgetting the grace of the upbeats. God is love and is more readily found in the upbeat though we must admit that the down beat is part of God's way, too. The passage this morning is full of grace; it is full of God and Jesus Christ and the Holy Spirit. The Holy Spirit is God present within us in a new way since Jesus Christ was born and died and rose again. And we are marked by that Spirit in our baptism, a graceful moment in our lives if there ever was one.

The rules for the new life are there to ensure that we stick close to the Spirit that dwells within us. When we are apart from that Spirit through failing to pay attention to the rules, we are out in the cold.

One way we stay close to God and are warmed by the light of God's love is to gather round this table for it reminds us that we belong to a God of grace and love. We are part of a family which has rules designed to result in harmony and growth.

    Eating together peacefully is a privilege which we too often take for granted. Having anyone to eat with is a plus in this life. It's what keeps the restaurant business alive. We like to eat together. We share something in common. If we have been careful to work hard at being kind and forgiving, at being honest and tenderhearted, we can eat the bread that is sustaining and eternal and it only add to our joy!

    This is the table of those who believe in the love shown forth in Jesus Christ, a love which we carry within us as baptized people. We are marked by the fact that the Holy Spirit dwells within us and the light of that spirit of love shines forth for all to see.

    The rules of the new life enable us to begin to be imitators of our God who loves us, and forgives us, and speaks the truth to us and shares with the needy - us. Yes, it is a love that we can only imitate in tiny ways but that is enough for now. To carry that kind of love is the sign of our being God's beloved children and together we can eat and share in the life of the Kingdom of God. Thanks be to God! Amen.

The Party's (Almost) Over
John 2:1-12

"Everyone serves the good wine first, and the inferior wine after the guests have become drunk. But you have kept the good wine until now."

When I was in high school, I was the band captain of our marching band. We were a very good band; in fact, we won marching competitions whenever we entered them. Twice we won the Greatest Band in Dixie contest in New Orleans during Mardi Gras. I'll never forget marching down Canal St. shoulder to shoulder with my comrades with the crowd pressing against the marchers at the end of each row so that we were like sardines. And people were throwing beads and coins from the sidewalk and trees and tops of buildings and the saxophone bells were filling up with loot which we divided up later among us. We wore straw hats and red blazers; a group made for Mardi Gras. It was a parade full of merry-making and we high-stepped along the road in pure triumph adored by thousands of people. We finished the parade high on affirmation and applause, bearing a very large golden trophy home on the Southern Crescent train, to Dalton, GA.

Such merry-making as that which took place all those years ago in New Orleans for a couple of weeks in February is a way of preparing for the somber time to come. Today is officially called Shrove Tuesday or in French, Mardi Gras, Fat Tuesday. At Mardi Gras time, the general theme is "Eat, drink and be merry for tomorrow we die." Today we eat, drink and be merry for tomorrow comes Ash Wednesday, and then we will have to fast and spend forty days repenting and thinking about our flawed mortal lives and the life of the tarnished world until we are redeemed at Easter.

The Old Testament is full of references to such merry-making as today brings. Some follow the theme of the wonderful passage from the book of Sirach. (Sirach 31:25-31) These proverbial sayings celebrate merry-making as part of human life and would be verses that the Mardi Gras crewes in New Orleans would endorse. At the same time - and this is something that even the revelers in the Big Easy would admit, along with Sirach - merry-making has a dark side, when wine is taken in excess and the results are harsh deeds and biting words. In the Old Testament, as part of the shadow side of merrymaking, the idea was usually to do somebody else in. "Wait until the king is deep in his merry-making then kill him." (II Samuel 13:28) Sometimes when people made merry too much, they did strange things, they were deceived, they were toppled from their thrones. Ecclesiastes following that theme in cynical fashion says to go ahead and make merry, have a good time for it will all end anyway in disaster and heartache due to human vanity. (Eccl 9:7-120

I asked my Catholic priest friend, Chris, if there was anything liturgical that the Catholics do on this day of Mardi Gras, Shrove Tuesday. His parish on Long Island is full of Italian, Irish and Polish Catholics for whom the tradition of merry-making before Lent is well known. He was intrigued by the question but could find no evidence of the church doing anything to guide the merry-making that precedes the first day of Lent. It seems that regular people through the centuries have come up with this way of celebrating furiously before they have to settle down and frown for the next forty days.

Have you ever frantically and intentionally celebrated before some ominous event?

We go out to eat the night before gum surgery.

We eat lots of peanut butter and chew pack after pack of bubble gum the week before the braces go on for a year or two.

This is also the impulse from which bachelor parties originated, along with the 90's version of that ritual which has the girls going to Chippendale's or Lemon Peel. There's something about human nature that demands an indulgent equalizing in advance of what we anticipate will be considerable pain.

Since there is no Biblical guidance for a chapel service on Mardi Gras day I thought of the story of the wedding at Cana as a possible way to look at celebration before solemnity, the first miracle of Jesus which starts him on the long and weary way to the cross. The wedding at Cana is a Biblical example of merry-making at its best. And because it is included in the gospel of John, the merrymaking and the water and the wine have the extra dimension of meaning more than one thing. The party and the miracle mean more than a simple tale of a wedding in a small village on a lazy afternoon and evening.

Jesus turns the water into wine at the height of the party when everybody's had a lot to drink already. If it's typical to start the party with Bordeaux, then switch to Boone's Farm when everybody's half snockered and won't notice the difference, then Jesus reversed the order of the pouring and did a surprising thing. This party starts out with some nice standard fare but when he does his miracle the vats turn out to be full of the finest champagne. I'm not a wine connoisseur so you can think of the best thing to drink and fill in the blank. I guess another analogy, this one involving bourbon, would be starting the party with Jack Daniels and switching to Thunderbird when nobody cares anymore. And yet, Jesus went from Jack Daniels to Woodford Reserve. Quite a wedding gift.

This may seem strange to you, this talk about liquor and the comparative merit of bourbon and wine in a chapel service, but it was a party after all and they were indeed serving wine, as they did throughout the Bible. One of my Disciple Bible study students grew up in the Baptist church and she said that the Baptists maintain that it wasn't wine at all that he turned the water into - it was grape juice. It only looked and smelled like wine. It doesn't really matter. What happened was that at the height of a nice party they were about to run out of refreshments and the festivities were about to grind to a halt. And this is what was being played out in the story of Jesus. His ministry is beginning and there will be much happiness because of the miracles, the signs and the good news he brings. But somewhere along the way it will all fall apart, and he will die. The wine will run out like blood at the foot of the cross. And yet that is not the end of the story.

Commentator Gerard Sloyan points out that in the Greek when "the wine failed" those words carried with them the connotation of something fairly predictable happening such as "when the sun rose" or "when the tide went out". At this wedding party where people are having a good time, the well has run dry. The bride's family has spent up the drink budget and the wine supply is now just so many honey-combed cardboard boxes tossed in the caterer's corner behind the banquet table, empty. There is no new wine to be had. Or so they think.

And so, Mary goes to her son and in Middle Eastern fashion simply states the problem - "they're out of wine." She doesn't demand that he do something. She doesn't say "look son, I'll just bet you can help these people out." She states the problem. Whereupon the two of them have a brief theological discussion before he relents and does even more than she asks. He uses the water vats set aside for ritual purification, directs them to be filled with water and behold when they draw it out now, it is new wine, the finest wine - enough for several parties and more than one Mardi Gras.

The partygoers have been able to find new life at its source. When the wine is gone, the blood has drained, and the life is gone from the party and from Jesus' life, he himself as God incarnate is the source of the renewal of life, both his and of the party which is human existence. Jesus himself is the purified living water as John will tell us later in the story of the Woman at the Well. But in this story of the wedding reception Jesus can provide the living water in the form of new wine. And who doesn't see that "living water" is as good a definition as any for fermented grapes carefully nurtured into liquid form, pleasant for merry-making. Jesus himself brings new life to the gathered friends and family.

The irony, of course, is that the party-goers don't even know what has happened. Only Mary and the disciples and Jesus are aware that a miracle has even taken place. It is a hidden thing he does which benefits the whole party. And this is only the beginning of the hidden nature of who Jesus is and what he means in our lives. Only later would those who witnessed or heard about this miracle, this sign, look back on it in wonder, and only later would John describe such an everyday event as a wedding, in terms that would rock the world. As Sloyan puts it, "To believe in Jesus as the Christ is to live a life within a life. Nothing is changed but everything is changed. What had been water is wine. Word has become flesh. An hour that has not yet come is here."

So on this Mardi Gras, Shrove Tuesday, the day before Lent

begins,

>we march jauntily along in the midst of the great parade

>we party down at the never-ending wedding reception that is 21st century America,

>and without even knowing it, without our even having a hint of what is to come, the proceedings are about to take a dramatic turn. "Eat drink and be merry," says Jesus, "for tomorrow you will truly begin to live."

The Luck of the Irish
Isaiah 58; John 7:37-39

"You shall be like a watered garden, like a spring of water whose waters never fail."

Like many other Americans I have an Irish ancestor. Her name was Hannah and she married an English man which was not the done thing just after Cromwell invaded Ireland and awarded land to English Puritans. My ancestor's husband, Daniel Candler, was the grandson of one of Cromwell's generals and when he committed the equally unpardonable sin of marrying an Irish woman, they were forced to leave Ireland and came to America. From this family thousands of descendants were born including the Coca-Cola Candlers and the less luminary Presbyterian, Cheryl Gosa.

Someday I want to go to Ireland and see the place where Hannah lived and try to understand what it must have been like to leave the land of her own ancestors and make her way to the New World, the pre-Revolutionary world of America in the early 1700's. My pioneer ancestors settled in Virginia first, then made their way south to Georgia and have been here ever since. This is all on my mother's side.

If you have read Frank McCourt's Pulitzer Prize winning book *Angela's Ashes* you know that the picture of the Irish as happy-go-lucky, leaping through shamrocks with leprechauns is false and misleading. Ireland has become while still devastatingly beautiful, a place where many people are still in the deepest poverty.

Nevertheless, there's something about Ireland and the Irish which-attracts us today, even if all we know is shamrocks and pots of gold at the end of the rainbow. Brigadoon is a place we want to experience even if in a dream.

St. Patrick was a real person and today we celebrate his day. He is the patron saint of Ireland along with St. Brigit, his female counterpart. Interestingly, St. Patrick wasn't even born in Ireland but was born about the year 390 AD on the west coast of England or Wales. His grandfather was a Christian priest indicating that

The Fire and the Knife

Christianity had been in the British Isles since very nearly the beginning of the faith. While Patrick was a youth he was kidnapped and taken to Ireland where he lived for six years as a slave herding sheep. When he eventually escaped and went back to England, he was inexplicably filled with a longing to become a priest and then to go back to Ireland as a missionary. So, when he was 42, after he had studied and been ordained in France, he returned to Ireland and became the most important figure in Irish Christian history. He died in Ireland at the age of 71 in 461 AD but no one knows exactly where he is buried. There are many legends about his death and fiery ascension into heaven.

Patrick though not Irish had no trouble at all becoming Irish in spirit. Perhaps because he spent part of his youth there, he absorbed the essence of the Irish Celtic spirit and preached in such a way that people heard him speaking their language. He was big and hearty and full of confidence. He walked among the people with good will and strong faith. He was larger than life, guided by dreams and visions which showed him the way.

It was St. Patrick who explained the Trinity to the Irish people by showing them a shamrock. Long before Christianity made it to that island, the people believed in a race of people who lived underground, a division of habitation brought about in mythological history by an agreement between those who originally lived in Ireland and those who came to live among them. The underground ones we now know as the leprechauns, the fairy folk.

The Celtic Christians were partial to the Old Testament because they had access to those manuscripts long before the New Testament ones made their way to the far reaches of the Christian world - their own island home. Their interest in Old Testament scripture though went beyond access to documents. The Celtic Christians believed in the goodness of creation, and the Old Testament is full of testimony to the goodness of what God had made. From Genesis through the prophets, they could read what they already knew, that God is present throughout creation, that in every rock and tree and bird and pool of water, God is there. From morning till night and every hour in between, God is present in everyday life. The world of the ancient Jew and the world of the early

The Fire and the Knife

Irish Christian was a world infused with God and God's blessings. Long before the gloomy view of totally depraved human nature which Augustine taught, the Irish knew a God and a human nature that was innately good. And while Irish Christians believed in sin, it was not original sin. Nobody is tainted at birth. We may choose to sin out of our free will, but we are not born incapable of acting rightly. We usually don't act rightly, in fact, as the human and biblical records abundantly show but nevertheless, thought the Celtic Christians, we could act rightly if we chose to. For this belief which many of us hold today, that we are born good, one Irish theologian named Pelagius was condemned as a heretic.

Isaiah, in this morning's text, beckons us in the name of God to "come to the waters, come buy and eat, even if you don't have money. Come buy wine and milk without money and without price." This kind of largess is called grace or in the translation of a contemporary commentator, kindness. God's kindness bids us to come and live abundantly. "Come to the place where the mountains and hills will burst into song where we will go out in joy and be led back in peace."

Likewise, in John, Jesus echoes this invitation telling the disciples "let anyone who is thirsty come to me and let the one who believes in me drink." And he quotes Isaiah saying, "out of the believer's heart shall come streams of living water." The abundance of life is shown to the hearers in the metaphor of food and drink, a satisfying life founded on the generosity of God.

Water holds a particularly important place in Irish cosmology. Before Christianity, the Old Religion venerated that which came from the earth, bringing life in the form of water. Water sustained, and it healed.

It was only a small step to readily accepting the idea of baptism as rebirth.

Trees were important to the Irish, too, and the oak especially held an important place in the interpretation of wisdom.

It was only a small step then to understanding the cross as

the combination of an oak tree and the savior outstretched upon its branches.

Irish mythology is full of high kings and triumphant leaders, shining princes and those who go down into the earth only to return blazing with sun.

It was only a small step in that case to accepting Jesus their brother, the same high king of heaven we sang about in the first hymn, the legendary one who went down into the underworld and returned in glorious splendor.

And the idea of bread and wine putting us in touch with the high king was an easy step for people who believed in the fruit of the earth and its power to link us with those who have gone before.

The Celtic cross is a picture of tree of life turned into a cross, encircled by the never-ending ring of creation, the endless view of time as not linear but a spiral where we meet those of a bygone age in the most ordinary of times.

If the Irish can be said to have luck, it is in their irrepressible strength and resilience in the face of almost impossible hardship. Out of windy hillsides, wading in freezing seas, living for years in small wooden huts, meditating in the solitude broken only by the cry of birds and the bleating of ever-present sheep, the Irish keep bouncing back, living on next to nothing and calling it bountiful. When the potato famine called so many to move to America, they made do with next to nothing and somehow flourished, partly from family and kinship ties, partly from an innate and ethnic belief that God is with us no matter how bad things look and God is calling it all good even if we can't imagine how.

On St. Patrick's Day I think about Hannah, my Irish ancestor, and think of her on a ship crossing the sea on pilgrimage, in exile for a decision made out of love, and see her as joining forces with those who, centuries before her, went out away from their homeland, never to return but always carrying Ireland in their hearts. I can almost see her valley and I believe I will recognize it when I get there. And I, too, carry a sense of the goodness of creation and the presence of God

> in each leaf, tree and flower,
>
> each cat and dog and caterpillar,
>
> each ocean and creek and river,
>
> not to mention each human being.

Can you hear God calling you this day to "come and eat, without price, without money, come all you who thirst and drink from the river of life, come enjoy the abundant life"? Whatever your life holds for you this day, it is a gift which may hide its joy right now, but it is there somehow shining like a pot of gold at the end of the rainbow which waits behind a cloud for the sky to clear.

Two Mosquitoes in Tokyo
John 12:1-8; Psalm 36

"For with you is the fountain of life; in your light we see light."

Did you know that the Hubbell telescope out in space is so powerful that if our eyes were as sensitive as its lens, then we, in Atlanta could actually see two mosquitoes in Tokyo? Now that's a marvelous thing to think about but as people of faith we know that seeing something takes place on more than one level. While the scientists are speaking about the telescope on a literal level in order to help us understand just how powerful that bit of machinery is up in space that the astronauts have to keep fixing, the poets would tell us on another level that seeing involves a lot more than optical acuity. Jesus himself often said "let those with eyes to see, see" and he didn't mean raise your eyelids and look.

Trying to really "see" the truth behind the facts of this text from thousands of years ago, to my mind, could be as difficult as trying to actually see two mosquitoes in Tokyo. But if we probe deeply enough with the eyes of our souls, we will be able to see one facet of the truth of what it means to be Christian.

The ballad that is Psalm 36 is the melody behind the lyrics in the gospel reading from John. Now and then we hear a song on the radio that tells the truth of love lost, more completely and profoundly than the toneless recounting of the chronological facts of any affair of the heart ever could. Psalm 36 speaks of the same reverence and deviousness that we find spelled out in the story in John's gospel. But in the Psalm, it is told in poetry and metaphor, which tell us far more than the facts. Poetry and metaphor have a way of telling us the truth.

Can you see Judas in the middle of the night staring at the ceiling, scheming about betrayal in the images of Psalm 36?

> "Transgression speaks to the wicked, deep in their hearts;
> they flatter themselves in their own eyes;
> they plot mischief while on their beds,

they are set on a way that is not good."

Can you see Mary drawing her hair across Jesus' feet and smelling the perfume that is drying and yet filling the room with its fragrance? Can you hear her singing her part of Psalm 36?

"How precious is your steadfast love, O God;
all people feast on the abundance of your house;
for with you is the fountain of life;
in your light we see light."

Psalm 36 is a song on two levels that shows us the truth in poetry that lies behind the facts of the narrative story in John. And in that blend of fact and truth, Judas echoes part one of Psalm 36 as surely as Mary echoes part two. And together they reflect the truth of being human.

In the gospel of John, Mary is giving a gift to a man she has come to love above all others. With fountains of love she anoints him. Meanwhile Judas on the other side of the table is brooding and calculating about the cost of the flagon of perfume, muttering about giving the money to the poor which is false piety since he really wants the money for himself. He flatters himself that he is looking out for the welfare of those less fortunate.

The poetry of Psalm 36 speaks of the two mosquitoes, if you will, of human treachery and devotion while the passage in John's gospel tells us a story about the facts of Judas and his metallic duplicity, of Mary and her perfumed love. It takes the eyes of faith to put them together and see the troth.

The truth of Mary's life was in the love she felt for Jesus which she embodied by the fact of falling down at his feet.

The truth of Judas' life was in the internal hypocrisy which he embodied by saying one thing and plotting another even as he sat at table with the one who saw everything.

The truth of our lives is in the *redemption* – **today** - that follows forgiveness for the things of the past.

The truth of our lives is in the *hope* that believes – **today** - in the future, whatever it holds.

The truth of our lives is in the *grace* that surrounds us – **today** - right now.

Not only are we dealing with the two mosquitoes of fact and truth, of deception and devotion; we are also trying to see the two mosquitoes of seeing and being seen.

Seeing and being seen are at the core of our faith. We are in relationship with God as creator, redeemer and sustainer in this moment, seeing and being seen, just as those friends gathered around the table were in relationship with Jesus, the man, at that moment.

And this ageless relationship is still held together today by God's steadfast love as shown to us in Jesus Christ and living within us as Holy Spirit. That same steadfast love which is sung in Psalm 36 is told anew in John's gospel as Jesus sat among them and loved them despite all he could see about them. We see God all around us and within us, with the eyes of faith and hope. And we are seen by God as who we are.

Jesus saw them all and loved them anyway.

God sees us all and loves us anyway.

The mixture of brooding and jubilance that Psalm 36 describes also describes each of us. God sees our own two mosquitoes of reverence and dishonesty and even so, they are mercifully surrounded by God's steadfast love. In God is the fountain of life and in God's light we see light.

As we come to this table this morning know that this is the truth which shall set us free.

To see God and to see each other, to be seen by God and

to be seen by each other, right now, despite all our fraud and in all our glory, with eyes of love and grace, gives us hope for the days which lie ahead. These elements of bread and wine are the means through which we can know that God is with us and will be forever. As the body of Christ gathered in this room this morning, we can be sure that he is among us.

Thanks be to God!

Into the Night
John 13:21-38; Psalm 88

"Are your wonders known in the darkness, or your saving help in the land of forgetfulness?"

Today is Wednesday of Holy Week; we are in the eye of the storm;

    the parade is over,

        the exhilaration has died down,

            the glow has faded,

                and the palm branches are beginning to wilt.

Tomorrow night is the familiar farewell banquet of Maundy Thursday, what we know in hindsight as the beginning of the end when the conclusion of the drama is set in motion.

John the gospel writer does not dwell on the Last Supper as we know it; in fact, he doesn't even mention it. John instead focuses on the foot washing on Thursday evening that precedes the meal and he follows that story with an equally intense episode. The lectionary text for today from the gospel of John is one in which we watch Jesus holding out the sacramental piece of bread to Judas as the dominoes begin to fall. The story of that fateful piece of bread reeks of betrayal and doubt just after Jesus has humbled himself to serve his followers and has directed them to go and do likewise. The Last Supper indeed goes explicitly unmentioned in John in the traditional way and yet in a very special way it is there.

Besides the obvious two characters of Jesus and Judas in this story, there is another player who not surprisingly gets in on the act - our old friend Peter who always wants to have the first and last words, who always blurts out whatever he feels, but who is also redeemed in the end from his guilt.

The Fire and the Knife

John the gospel writer loves to make points by focusing on individual people and what happens to them in relation to Jesus and this story is no exception. So, we have Jesus, Judas and Peter who will all soon be singing Psalm 88, each in his own key, at his own time, each with his own knowledge, each with his own faith and uncertainty.

After the foot washing is over, John tells us that Jesus is troubled in spirit and declares that one of the disciples will betray him.

- Can you imagine the shock they feel?

- Are they frozen like deer caught in the headlights, as still as mice so as not to call attention to themselves?

- Do they stop chewing?

- Do they swallow that wine with a gulp? Who me?

- Do they each one rapidly replay their mental tapes for any sign of betraying Jesus?

Certainly not Peter. Peter can't contain himself and not content to leave well enough alone and let things unfold as they surely will, he nudges his friend, John, saying "Ask him who he means. He'll tell you, he likes you best."

Put yourself at that table for a moment and try to forget everything you know about the events of Holy Week yet to come. Jesus is a miracle worker; he seems to be able to read minds. He talks in parables and riddles. What is he talking about and who is he talking about? Could I be the one? Surely not.

Judas is quiet in the story. But Peter certainly wants to know "who dunnit," he wants to hear who the villain is, he wants to go after the guy. He wants to make sure he isn't the one, when you and I know perfectly well that it is - on down the road. So, the one whom Jesus loved best, namely John, asks Jesus "who is it?" .... and in that dramatic pause before Jesus answers can't you see him looking at each one of them with overwhelming love and compassion?

In the silence of the room with
    people calling outside the window,
    donkeys braying,
    music playing,
    the sounds of the street,
    the gathered heat and dusty smell of the day's end,
    the tallow of the burning candles,
    the wine and the remains of the feast.
it is a real E.F. Hutton moment.

And Jesus picks up a little piece of bread and declares that the betrayer will be the one to whom he hands the bread. And he dips it in the dish of oil, an intinction that holds a turning point in the life of one man and of all. I imagine he takes his time as they wait breathless. He holds out that piece of bread and turns around the circle with his eyes once more, pausing at each person, before stopping at Judas, handing it to him saying "Do quickly what you are going to do.

And Judas takes the piece of bread from Jesus' hand.

- Does he eat and run?

- Does he throw it down in his haste to be away?

- Does he eat it slowly, never taking his eyes from Jesus?

- Has he, as Barbara Brown Taylor posits, simply fallen out of love with Jesus?

- Is Judas' taking of the bread from Jesus' hand a kind of sacrament of what he is about to do?

- Is Jesus handing his own body into the care of Judas?

- Is Judas merely a robot, taken over by Satan, unable to keep from betraying Jesus even if he had wanted to?

The Fire and the Knife

- Or does he do what he does out of love, with some sense that he must do it for us all to have Easter morning and the resurrection? John does not answer any of these questions, only telling us that Judas received the bread and went out and it was night.

John does not tell us what happens to Judas after the betrayal later that night in the garden - John will simply never speak of him again. Like a disinherited son whose name is never spoken again at home, Judas will be dead to John whether he kills himself or not, as one of the other gospel writers relates. And the other disciples watch Judas in wonder as he goes forth from that upper room. What is he going to do? How will he betray the Master?

Judas receives from the hand of Jesus what we will forever see through our Christian sacramental eyes as Jesus' body symbolized in a piece of bread. "This is my body," says Jesus to Judas as we imagine the familiar words, "which will be broken for you. Do this thing which you are going to do, quickly, remembering me." And Judas goes out into the night. And when he does what he has set out to do does he cry out to God in the song of the 88th Psalm:

> *"O Lord God, my soul is full of troubles.*
> *I am counted with them that go down into the pit.*
> *I am as a man that hath no strength*
> *Thou hast laid me in the lowest pit, in darkness, in the deep.*
> *Thy wrath lieth hard upon me.*
> *Thou hast put away mine acquaintances far from me;*
> *Thou hast made me an abomination unto them.*
> *Lord, why castest thou off my soul? I am afflicted and ready to die".*

Well, that was Judas. We would surely never betray Jesus in such a profound and dramatic way, we think. Jesus picked up a little piece of bread and declared that the betrayer would be the one to whom he handed the bread.

And he dipped it in the dish of oil;

he took his time as they waited breathless,

he held out that piece of bread and turned around the circle with his eyes once more before stopping.

I'll bet you could hear a pin drop in that upper room for a few seconds anyway after Judas had hurried out. "At least he passed over me", they all think in great relief, especially Peter, but what in the world does Jesus mean - do it quickly? Do what quickly? Then the buzz starts as they try to figure out what Judas is up to and what Jesus meant.

Where Judas was single-minded, Peter is adaptable. He moves on with Jesus into the new topic of discussion that follows Judas' departure and now he boldly makes his vows of love and discipleship. "I would lay down my life for you," Peter declares in bravado and extroverted conviction.

Can you just see Jesus then with that same look of love and compassion as he says- "oh my friend, what do you know of laying down your life?" And softly he says to Peter, "you will deny me not once but three times before it is all over."

We know the gospel stories so well that we blend them all together. Our minds synthesize the story that follows. We know that Peter indeed will betray Jesus, deny ever knowing him, three times, and he will break down and weep as he remembers Jesus words. Jesus was right, and we remember the prediction. It will be less than twelve hours from the time of this upper room story until Peter betrays Jesus in his own way.

In the night, that same night, Peter will betray his friend and he will go down into the dark night of his own soul. And the guilt will only get worse for him as the horror of Friday turns into the numbness of Saturday's tomb. The blackness will go on and on for Peter until his redemption on the beach following Easter. But for now, in a kind of time warp, we can hear Peter vowing around the supper table to lay down his life for Jesus and simultaneously we can see the scene the very next dawn in the courtyard, like a split screen on TV, as Peter agonizes over what he, too, will have done to Jesus.

"O Lord God of my salvation, let my prayer come before thee.

For my soul is full of trouble.

I am as a man that hath no strength.

Shall thy wonders be known in the dark? and thy righteousness in the land of forgetfulness?

I am afflicted and ready to die from my youth up. Thy fierce wrath goeth over me; thy terrors have cut me off.

Lover and friend hast thou put far from me and mine acquaintance is in darkness."

And so, we are left with Jesus, the third character in the story. He picks up a little piece of bread and declares that the betrayer will be the one to whom he hands the bread. And he dips it in the dish of oil, he takes his time as they wait breathless, he holds up that piece of bread and turns around the circle with his eyes once more before stopping ...

Putting aside all the theological questions about what he knew when and what he set aside in order to be human, we know that Jesus was a man of high intuition about others and surely about himself. He can see the writing on the wall; things are getting hot. Politics surround him, and he is walking slowly but surely into the fire. And yet he follows God even then and in his fear of what is to come, with courage surmounting any the world has ever known, he plays out the hand that has been dealt to him - one disciple betraying him publicly in a flurry of glinting swords and silver pieces; another betraying him privately in the shadows of a courtyard campfire.

- Trials and questions and pain and humiliation.

- Abandonment and suffering without measure.

But that is yet to come. In the stillness of the night after the Last Supper he tries to tell his friends what they need to know after he is gone. He knows he is going to die, and he knows that somehow, he is going to live again, for God has told him so - in the prophets of the holy scripture he has learned so well, and in the prayer times he has so cherished. But he also knows Psalm 88 and the despair and blackness that life sometimes can become, and he must wonder if he, too, will feel that kind of terror of the night.

> *"O Lord God of my salvation let my prayer come before thee.*
>
> *Incline thine ear to my cry. for my soul is full of trouble and my life draweth nigh to the grave.*
>
> *Wilt thou show wonders to the dead?*
>
> *Shall the dead arise and praise thee?*
>
> *Shall thy loving-kindness be declared in the grave or thy faithfulness in destruction?*
>
> *Shall thy wonders be shown in the darkness?*
>
> *Lover and friend hast thou put far from me, and mine acquaintance in the night.*

Judas, Peter, Jesus. But what of us? Jesus holds out a piece of bread and shows it to us all and he gives it to each of us, each one of us who will always do what we must do, for we are only human.

- What will we do when the darkness surrounds us, and the terrors come round about us like mighty waters?

- What will we do when we walk into the darkness of guilt and betrayal?

- What will we do when he extends his hand to us, the piece of bread that is his body given into our care?

- Will we wait, considering, like Judas, whether we will take it?

- Will we accept it easily, believing ourselves, like

Peter, fully capable of standing up for Jesus under the strongest of stress?

When we hold that bread in our hands, walking down into the darkness of our own night, will we cherish it, remember it, feel it changing into us as we take it into ourselves?

From his hand to ours, we take the body of Christ and hold it close, knowing as we do, that in the sad darkness of the next three days lies the seed of the triumph we will feel come Sunday morning. Over and over throughout our lives, we will indeed betray him, an endless repeat that, try as we might, we cannot stop. For we are Judas and we are Peter with betrayals large and small of that Christ which is within us.

But as we go down into the darkness of this weekend, let us wait with Christ Jesus for the impossible transformation that he promised would be ours, too, Through the power of the Holy Spirit, we, too, will rise from the depths of the night into the light, not only on Easter morning but each time we stumble in the darkness and find ourselves led back into the day by the grace of a forgiving and ever loving God.

John's story of denial and betrayal foretold - a story that will culminate in grace untold - this is the story we hear each time we celebrate what we call the Last Supper. Tomorrow, on Maundy Thursday, as you eat and drink with those believers gathered around you in the night, remembering Christ and his sacrifice, receive the bread from his hand and see the mercy and compassion on his face yet again.

For he knows our darkness as well as he knows our light. He knows our intent as well as he knows our fully human nature. And he knows that our very best efforts and our very biggest failures are all encompassed in a piece of bread extended to us with love across the ages. "Do what you will, always remembering me."

Thanks be to God for grace outpoured in Jesus Christ. Amen.

A Double Share
II Kings 2:1-14; Luke 9:51-62

"Please let me inherit a double share of your spirit."

Did you ever want to know Jesus as a man?

Did you ever want to see him do a miracle?

Did you ever want to feel the touch of his hand?

Did you ever just want to walk with him on hot and dusty roads in the noonday sun or at twilight?

Wouldn't you feel so special if as you walked along the road, he threw his arm around you or clapped you on the shoulder or passed you a morsel of fish or a fig, a cup of wine, a piece of bread.

What a joy to be with him like that!

There must have been something about him that drew people to him, that made people want to follow him anywhere. Don't you think he had the ability to make people sit up and take notice, to be held by his eyes, unable to let go until he was finished with what he was saying? And I'll bet they could remember his words long after he was gone and rehearse his sermons and his sayings and his jokes.

Both scripture passages we read this morning talk about this kind of relationship between teachers and students, between masters and disciples, between mentors and learners. It is the kind of relationship that we know about, too, at one time or another in our lives, the special relationship that draws us in, that makes us want to do anything to be near the one we love and admire.

That is also the kind of relationship that, at its best, we want to have with God - an all-consuming involvement that will last forever. A kind of being "in love" that makes us better people than we usually are, that makes us love life and the world and everybody in it, that makes us want to give away some of the love we have received in such abundance.

In the Old Testament passage this morning, Elisha certainly felt that way about Elijah. He kept following Elijah down the road as they journeyed, refusing to turn back, refusing to let go, refusing to say goodbye even when Elijah said it was time for him to go away.

And then Elijah came to the river and hit the water with his coat and a passage was made for them to walk across on dry land. And on the other side of the river, as the moment of parting neared, Elijah offered Elisha a wish, a favor, and Elisha in anguish blurted out a request - for a double share of Elijah's spirit.

Can you feel what he was asking for?

> He wanted not to be abandoned.

> He wanted to feel Elijah's presence more than ever.

> He wanted Elijah's wisdom and power.

> He wanted to be free of whatever bound him in life, free to go the way God would have him go and to do the work in the world which God had created him to do.

The condition for receiving the wish was precise. Elijah vowed to Elisha that if he didn't take his eyes from him as God took him up into heaven, he'd get his wish. If he could just hang on and not be distracted and watch Elijah all the way, he'd get what he asked for.

And so Elisha with dry eyes, unblinking, frozen open, watched Elijah go. And when he had entirely vanished, like your own beloved down the airport jetway onto the plane and he could no longer see even a fragment of Elijah's hair or clothing,

Elisha stood alone in the quiet and Elijah was gone.

Can you see him then picking up Elijah's discarded cloak, a souvenir that was familiar, that smelled like Elijah maybe, trudging slowly back to the river and in dejection slapping it on the water sobbing "where is Elijah's God, the one he told me over and over to trust and who would never leave me? If I can't have Elijah anymore, then I want to have God." And look, the river parts, proof that Elisha has gotten his wish. Elijah's spirit is with him abundantly, overflowing, the double share he asked for.

Jesus said the same thing, in effect, to his disciples. If you keep your eyes on the Kingdom of God and don't look back, you will make it. But the disciples didn't last long with their eyes on the prize, did they? We can hear some of the same feeling of the Elisha story in the post-Easter accounts of the disciples, dejected, hiding in upper rooms, full of gloom and doom after Jesus had been crucified.

And yet Jesus had told them that on Pentecost just weeks later they were going to receive a double portion of the Spirit of Christ, enough to last their whole lifetime and all the way down to ours.

The fact of the matter is that we, too, individually and as the Body of Christ have received a double portion of Holy Spirit from God. We are born with God's spirit within us, it is what gives us life. When God breathes the spirit of life into us, we live. When God takes away that spirit, we die. That is part of being human. But the double share is something extra.

As Christians we have a double share of spirit - that spirit with which we were born plus that spirit which we realize that we have received as children of God at our baptism into the Body of Christ.

If we can keep our eyes on Christ;

if we can keep our eyes open and focused on what God would have us do;

if we can keep from looking away from what
God is showing us every day of our lives,

then we will continue to know that we have received more than enough of the Holy Spirit to last our whole life and more, and then we can go about the business of God's Kingdom full of hope and confidence and love - like Elisha, like the disciples of Jesus.

But what exactly does it mean for us to have the gift of a double share of Christ's spirit? And how is that different from just having our fair share, our due as human beings?

I

First, I think having a double share of God's spirit means having a double share of the presence of God in our lives and in the life of the church. The idea of presence is an important one and we can understand it best by putting it in human terms.

When you are present to someone it means that when you are with her, she has your undivided attention. When you are present to someone it means that you listen to her carefully, that you support her and affirm her, that you are her cheerleader, you believe the best about her. To be present is to be beside someone, not necessarily doing anything, but just being there because your very presence means comfort and love. Silent presence is often much more comforting than words or thoughts or advice anyway.

When someone is present with you, you know he understands, he has been there, he knows how you feel; she knows you are feeling terrible or sad or lonely and she wants to be with you even if it is just sitting there holding your hand. And you find great comfort in that kind of presence. When the church is present for someone in need, and when we are present when the church is in need, we are representing the presence of God to each other and to the world.

In the same way, God, through the Holy Spirit whom Jesus Christ sent us, is present with us, a loving presence

> that feels with us and for us,
>
> that hopes for the best for us,

that comforts us without words,

that knows how we are feeling and is happy

or sad or angry or fearful with us.

And that portion of Spirit, that extra share of God's presence with us is something we can rely on always.

Think about the times when you have felt God's presence in your life because someone was there for you, loving you no matter what.

Think about the times when you have felt God's presence in your life because someone helped you at an opportune moment, spoke a word of support or comfort that was for you alone.

Think about the times when you have felt God's presence in the steadfast love reflected in the eyes of a child.

Think: about the times when you have felt God's presence all around you

in the quiet mercy of a snow fall,

as the rain pours down the driveway,

as the sun pierces the curtains of your room
early in the morning.

These are all proof of the double share of the spirit of the presence of God which we have received. And if you have lost sight of these times, then pray fervently, for God wants us to know that we do have a double share of this presence. And like Elisha we have only to focus on receiving it. The miracle of the Good News of Jesus Christ is that if we can open our eyes and our hearts, if we can watch, we will see that we have it already.

It is called grace. It is love that never runs out, that is always present, always fresh and new and is always just right for who we are and where we are in our lives. Grace, a double share of God's presence, means that not only can we feel God inside us, comforting us, but we can also feel God all around us in the actions and words and sheer presence of other people acting on behalf of God. And we can be that kind of presence to others as well.

II

The second thing it means to have a double share of God's spirit is to know an abundance of wisdom. All of us as human beings have the capacity to reason, to observe, to analyze, to make judgments and wise decisions - some more so than others. But Jesus said that the Holy Spirit would guide us all into the truth. Discerning the truth, the right way to go is often the hardest thing we have to do. In any given situation we wonder what the right direction is, we flounder around trying to detect the answers for ourselves or for somebody else, we sit in the dark and wonder where the light at the end of the tunnel is.

Have you ever just wanted to know the right answer? Wouldn't it be nice to get e-mail from God? "Dear Cheryl, here is what I want you to do next. Step one, step two, step three. Talk to you later. Love, God." Or wouldn't it be nice to trust that the person you love the best could come to you and you would know for sure that their advice is straight from God. "Honey, God said for me to tell you this."

But that's too easy, isn't it? And yet in any case, only when we are silent long enough to listen - as individuals and as the church - can we discern with the wisdom that the Holy Spirit brings, what course we should follow or whether we should just wait and be patient, or whether we should stop what we have planned. A double share of the Spirit of wisdom is an almost overwhelming proposition but it is available to us because Jesus said it would be. The Holy Spirit which Christ promised is more than enough, it is there every moment of every day guiding us and directing us with wisdom toward the truth.

III

The third thing it means to have a double share of God's spirit is to live freely. For all our history as human beings, we have been part of various systems of rules and regulations, the meticulous keeping of which guaranteed salvation and a right ordering of the world. By adjusting our rituals and ceremonies we could restore the balance of the cosmos and do God's will ever more effectively.

But as human beings we get carried away with rules, and the keeping of those rules can turn into obsessive compulsive behavior. If you saw the movie "As Good as it Gets" you know about Jack Nicholson's ritual for locking and unlocking the front door. Remember that? Don't laugh too hard.

I'll bet you have your own ritual for locking your house at night. I can't leave my house in the morning without going through a certain set of actions in a certain order which reassure me that the stove is off, and the coffee pot is unplugged. The rules and regulations which make us feel safe, give us a feeling of freedom for the rest of the day.

Well God did us one better. God became human in order to show us that we are truly free now to live and love. We don't have to die and be rewarded with a crown or a halo in heaven to be secure that God has freed us. We are free now from deriving our safety and reassurance from keeping the rules correctly. We are free now because of grace, because we can see that in Jesus Christ - his life and death and resurrection, - we have received a double share of God's spirit.

> By grace we can get up in the morning and know that we are fine just the way we are.

> By grace we can walk into our offices and know that no matter what decisions we make, our value as people is intact.

> By grace we can sit down to take an exam at school and know that even if we don't ace the test and get into the number one college on our list, we are still OK and nevertheless have great potential in life.

The Fire and the Knife

The key is to live knowing about this gift of grace and to be grateful for it and then to give back to others the love we are getting from God. The freedom to live knowing we are surrounded by love is heady stuff indeed. And yet that is what the disciples had, whether they felt it or not. They were with Jesus for three years, day in and day out; they were surrounded by the love of God, literally, throughout every day.

Did they feel it enough? Did they value enough the freedom bound up in that love?

Did they know as they grieved his death that in fact, they had been in love with him, dazzled by his presence, his wisdom, the freedom he brought into their lives despite the dangers and the perils?

Did they know?

Did they know at Pentecost that he was with them again, doubly so now, as Holy Spirit; that because he was gone, he was able to be even more present with them, offering them wisdom and freedom to love as God had always loved them?

I think some of them did. I think some of them were aware of what was happening to their hearts. But others of them were caught up in their heads, trying to figure out the parables and make sense of the sermons and continue to carefully follow the rules. And in so doing, they missed the magic, the joy, the wonder of being in the presence of God – every day.

There is some magical quality to knowing this double share of God's spirit in all its forms. It is sort of like being in love, that feeling which makes life bright and new and exciting every moment. That feeling that the future is ahead of us and anything can happen.

Do we feel the Spirit within us and around us enlivening us and leading us into creative and inventive places as individuals and as the church?

Do we live like Elisha who even though he had just lost his

best friend, was miraculously able to carry on Elijah's legacy?

Do we feel the overwhelming comfort and security of the double share we have been given of God's presence?

Do we acknowledge the beginning of wisdom which comes from having a double portion of the Spirit of Christ?

Do we feel free enough to stand on a mountaintop and proclaim our love for this God who loved us enough to become human?

If we don't feel it, we need to pray that our hearts will open to recognize what is already there. If we don't think that's possible, we need to read our Bibles again. If we don't want to take a chance on the power and the passion that comes from having the double share of God's spirit that is ours, then we need to go to a quiet place and have a reckoning with God because God wants us to know that we do indeed have a double share of spirit, an abundance of grace. But why do we have it anyway? Because God wants us to give it to somebody else. We have it in order to pass it on.

It won't run out; we'll always have more and more and more. And the whole point is to give it away so that we will have more.

The whole point is that other people need to know about this great gift, too.

The whole point is that we are living in love with Jesus Christ and we just can't help spreading the news that love surrounds us and it is free for the taking.

The whole point is that God is love, that the Holy Spirit is presence and wisdom and freedom and those are the fruits of God's grace.

The whole point is that God comes running to us, giving us a whole world full of love.

And when we live daily in that kind of passionate love with Jesus and with God and with the presence of the Holy Spirit, we cannot keep it to ourselves and we cannot treat each other with anything other than kindness and honesty and openness.

God's gift of grace, that double share of spirit, is that as Christians we have more than enough love to share, that we can live our lives like people in love always, whether or not there is a human being that we are currently practicing on.

For you see, to be in love with another person is to act out, to demonstrate, to symbolize the steadfast love which God has for us.

To be in love with life is to care about the world as God cares for the whole of creation.

To be in love with God is to yearn for closeness and oneness, to reach for that bright light which sees us through each day and each night.

A double share of God's spirit is like

>a huge slice of angel food cake,

>an ocean sized vat of living water that quenches thirst,

>a sky full of spiritual richness and passion.

A double share of God's spirit means presence and wisdom and freedom - the ingredients for lives of love and mercy that reflect God's grace to every person we meet. Jesus knew what he was talking about when he told his disciples to keep their eyes on the kingdom. It's a sight worth seeing.

Elisha knew what he was doing when he kept his eyes on his friend and he knew what he was asking for, because only a double share of spirit would see him through the rest of his life without Elijah, and he knew he had better be careful what he asked for - he just might get it. And so, my friends, might we. Amen.

Holy Ground
Exodus 1:22-2:10, 3:1-5; John 20:11-16,18a

"Remove the sandals from your feet, for the place on which you are standing is holy ground."

The two episodes from the early life of Moses - the voyage through the bulrushes and the encounter with the burning bush - and the story of Jesus appearing to Mary in the garden on Easter morning, are familiar stories to us all. From early Sunday School and Bible School-days we learned the exciting story of how the baby was set sail in a little boat and discovered by the Pharaoh's daughter and how his little sister was able to save her brother and have him raised by their own mother. And we were awed by the story of the burning bush that didn't burn up and God talked to Moses there. As adults we came to appreciate the idea of Jesus actually appearing to a devoted friend after being dead for three days. Today I want to focus on the concept of holy ground that is present in all three stories.

We meet God in many ways. We communicate with God and God communicates with us through prayer, in dreams, in the words of other people, through music, through beautiful sights. And when we encounter God through any of these things, we say we're on holy ground.

The Bible gives us the term "holy ground" in this story of the adult Moses. He was out walking one day and out of the corner of his eye he saw a bush burning as if with fire. The Bible says an angel was in the bush causing it to burn in order to get Moses' attention. And Moses decided to check it out, this unusual phenomenon. He went over for a closer look. Then the Bible says that once the angel had gotten Moses' attention, God spoke from the bush calling Moses' name. Moses answered and then God said this is holy ground. The voice went on to describe who God was and Moses was afraid to look at God and hid his face.

It is awesome indeed to hear the voice of God. Some of you may have the experience of having heard it. Contrary to popular belief it is not only ministers who are supposed to be able to hear

The Fire and the Knife

God calling. Many people hear the voice of God and as a matter of fact many ministers can't claim any kind of definitive audibly verbal call. God speaks in ways that each individual can hear best. Evidently Moses required a visual cue and verbal information. But this was not the first holy ground in Moses' life. For that we have to go back to his birth, before it, in fact. The Pharaoh, fearing Israelite power, had decided to kill all the boy babies and allow the girl babies to live thus keeping the Hebrew population under control. Moses' mother found a way to save her son. The water of the river was holy ground for it cradled the tiny boy who would grow up to save his people. The naming of Moses by the Pharaoh's daughter is a play on the Hebrew words. She said I will call him Moses - "mosheh" for I drew him out "mosheh', of the water. Mosheh, child of holy ground.

The parallels between this Old Testament story and the Christian story are interesting. As Christians the waters of baptism are the holy ground out of which we become part of the household of faith. Out of the water we rise to belonging as Moses was drawn out of the water into the household of the Pharaoh, the safe, protected place from which a leader grew to adulthood. Jesus' life, too, was threatened as an infant by the powers that be and he, too, was divinely protected by being sent to Egypt until he was old enough to survive on his own.

Moses would have his own epiphany, his encounter with God, as a young man at the burning bush. Jesus would hear his call in the wilderness as he fasted and sweltered in the desert heat. And we all have this kind of epiphany at one time or another when we reach the individual conclusion that God has put us here for a purpose and that no matter where we go we cannot find our way to a place where God is not. For spiritual pilgrims Psalm 139 puts it quite poetically and comfortingly: "If I take the wings of the morning and settle at the farthest limits of the sea, even there your hand shall lead me, and your right hand shall hold me fast."

All of us arise from holy ground. Some of us may have been literally plucked from the bulrushes, saved from a childhood of danger and abuse by the hand of salvation. For some, holy ground was the shaky ground of neglect transformed by a child herself into a solitary hiding place of refuge. On the other hand, perhaps we were nurtured in the waters of a loving family. Perhaps the holy ground of our childhood church gave us a firm foundation to stand on as we grew to adulthood.

What makes the ground holy, of course, is God's presence. And because, as even the youngest child knows - God is everywhere - then holy ground is all around us.

God was covertly but solidly there in the bulrushes with baby Moses.

God was blatantly, visibly there in the burning bush for grownup Moses.

God is visibly there for us every day in the sunrise, in a flower, a baby's smile.

And God is covertly there repeatedly as we remember our origins and the places where God was working anonymously to bring us to the place where now we stand.

But there is another place where God always is and that is the holy ground of our souls.

Our souls are the part of us that speaks God's language naturally. There need be no translation for the benefit of our brains. There need be no overt signs or words that our minds understand and logically decipher. The soul speaks the language of symbol, which is non-verbal, paradoxical, feeling, circular, intuitive, "a deep but dazzling darkness" according to 17th century poet Henry Vaughan. He saw the mystery of God as darkness, as seeing in a mirror dimly, but also as an irresistible fire.

> "There is in God, some say,
> A deep but dazzling darkness, as men here
> Say it is late and dusky, because they
> See not all clear."

There is fire there indeed and when we are near to the fire, we are near to the divine. The holy ground of the soul is fertile and colorful; it soars through timeless space, it seeks union with God, like seeking like. It is the paradox of the soul's holy ground being placeless and timeless yet embodied in human form that makes the life of the soul so compelling. We can't put our finger on it, we can't find it on a map. But we know it is there as surely as we know the name of the town where we were born and can name the items in the cigar box of treasures we kept as a child.

But sometimes we need something we can put our finger on to contrast with this elusive soul which is not tangible. Anne Morrow Lindbergh put it this way in a poem, this concept of what is present but intangible, of formless space being real and yet perceptible only in relation to something else:

"A tree's significant when it's alone.
Standing against the sky's wide-open face;
A sail, spark-white upon the space of sea,
can pin a whole horizon into place.
Encompassed by the dark, a candle flowers,
creating space around it as it towers,
Giving the room a shape, a form, a name;
Significance is born within the frame.
A word falls in the silence like a star,
Searing the empty heavens with the scar
of beautiful and solitary flight.
Against the dark and speechless space of night."

Many of you have heard Rev. Jerry Wright speak of the story "The Golden Tree". In that story a king and a queen have a vision of a beautiful tree that is dazzling, that shines blindingly with leaves of gold and blossoms of diamond. It is difficult to look on this tree directly, but it is compelling. They can't help but search for it. The king and the queen relentlessly pursue the golden tree of their dreams and when they find it, they are joined to their real life, they are home, they begin to live happily ever after together.

Of course, interpreting this story for its meaning in our own lives, the king and queen represent the whole of ourselves, the golden tree represents the soul, and the soul is our link to the divine. Moses found his golden tree in the wilderness, a tree that burned with a flame but was not consumed. He grew up in the Pharaoh's household, was raised to be a leader, was well versed in the ways of the land but he had to find his own soul to begin to take on the unique task of his life. He had to be joined to a sure knowledge of the divine to get on with his work. All of his education, all of his cultured upbringing, all of his language studies and diplomas prepared him well for life, but the preparation was not complete without this encounter with God, this establishing of holy ground which would be with him forever after and provide the foundation for his life.

There comes a time and a place where we realize that the ground is indeed holy, when we have an encounter with the deep darkness at our core and where we recognize who and whose we are. Moses was afraid to look at God, knowing full well that it was God who was speaking with him.

In the New Testament after Jesus' resurrection, Mary was at the tomb. Again, an angel prepared the way for her encounter with her soul's desire. The angels tell her Jesus is not there. She roams the garden searching, searching for her friend. She sees a man, she thinks it's the gardener. She asks him where Jesus is. He calls her name "Mary." And she recognizes him and runs to tell the disciples, saying "I have seen the Lord."

God called "Moses" and he met God. Jesus called "Mary" and she knew Jesus. The difference in these two stories is that Moses was afraid to look at God and Mary told everybody she had seen the Lord. Moses was not yet ready to take on the identity of God's chosen one. There were a few more messages that had to come from God before he was willing to do the task to which he had been born. Mary had come through the fire of losing her best friend and it was as natural as hearing to recognize his voice despite her awe that a dead man was actually speaking to her. Both Moses and Mary were walking on the holy ground of an encounter with God.

Moses eventually learned through a series of mighty acts of God to trust what he was afraid to see. The Christ in Mary, the same Christ within each of us, called to her and her soul recognized the call. Mary relied on her own life, her feelings for Jesus that caused her to seek Him, to lay claim to this Lord who was the same and yet now very different. Her instinct was to go to him, to touch him. But theirs was to be a different relationship. It was now the holy ground of soul on which they would meet.

I have been thinking about what Jesse Sasser said a couple of weeks ago when he talked to us about the Focus weekend on spiritual disciplines coming up soon. He quoted someone as saying that we are not human beings seeking a spiritual experience, but we are spiritual beings seeking a human experience. I think that is indeed true; we are at heart spiritual beings seeking human experience. But the further truth is that we are both human and spiritual and always seek the opposite experience, that which will complete us. And yet all of us all are wired differently.

Some of us need the concrete first, what we can touch and objectify, to know that something is real or true. Others of us most readily know by our feelings, our intuition. God has provided for all kinds of people. Holy ground is widely defined in the geography of God.

If you need to see endless vistas in the Appalachian Mountains to notify your soul that you are on holy ground, God will lead you there.

If you need to feel a warm dark fire glowing in your inner self that only your heart sees, then God will keep it stoked.

What is magical about all this is that all of us need both kinds of holy ground. We need both the sensory power of the endless mountain vista and the intangible inner dark fire of the soul. It's just easier to begin one way or the other for most of us.

And that is what our formal worship is based on - this human need for more than one kind of evidence of the warmth of God's love and the fire of God's power. For this is the holiest of ground - that time when we set our souls and minds to worship the One who created, redeemed and sustains us. Whether it is here in this place, at home at our private altars, or there in small groups among friends and fellow pilgrims - we have the furniture, the food, and the feelings of holy ground. The colors, the sounds, the smells, the textures, and the tastes are provided for not only our bodies but for our souls as well. We are body and soul together, we are holy ground, inside and out.

We need the colors of stained glass and candlelight, but also the interior colors of joy and longing;

we need the sounds of trumpets and bells, but also the sounds of adoration and whispered love;

we need the smells of incense and evergreens, but also the smells of the fire of heaven and the wafting perfume of angels' wings;

we need the textures of paper and wood but also the feel of everlasting arms and the kiss of peace;

we need the taste of bread and wine but also the taste of eternal life and the waters of the fount of every blessing.

This is holy ground, we are holy ground. Our worship outward and inward is what keeps us close to the Source, the fire, the well of living water. The honoring of our bodily needs and our spiritual needs together, keeps us down to earth but at the same time also helps us escape into the ecstatic boundlessness of inner space.

Take off your shoes for you are standing on holy ground. Your very human feet walk daily on holy earthly ground and at the same time your immortal soul rides the wings of the morning's holy ground that you can never see with human eyes, but can only experience in the warm darkness of God's eternal love. In the name of the Father, the Son and the Holy Spirit, Amen.

Secret Heart
Psalm 51

"You desire truth in the inward being; therefore, teach me wisdom in my secret heart."

Before I read the scripture for today, I need to set the stage, to remind us of the story that leads up to the writing of Psalm 51. If you remember, one day King David was walking on the roof of the palace and in the garden of the house next door was a beautiful woman named Bathsheba. David fell in love with her on sight and had her brought to the palace. Bathsheba liked him, too. There was only one problem. Bathsheba was already married to a soldier named Uriah, currently off at the wars. But this was easily remedied. King David arranged for Uriah to be sent to the front line for the next battle and in due time he died as expected. Now David and Bathsheba could be together legally, if not morally.

The prophet Nathan heard about this incident and went to the King. "Your majesty, I have a story for you. There was once a poor man who had only one sheep. He took good care of it, he loved it, he treated it as part of his family. Next door to him lived a wealthy farmer with a whole flock of sheep. One day some important people came to dinner and rather than kill one of his own sheep, the wealthy man sent someone next door to commandeer the poor man's only sheep which he promptly served for supper. I ask you, your majesty, what should be done about this rich man?" David was incensed and said "why, he should be strung up, he has done a terrible thing." Nathan pointed to the king and said "You, sir, are that man." David got the point immediately and went away sorrowfully. And in the depths of his despair he sat down and wrote Psalm 51.

Not too long ago in the "Atlanta Constitution" there was a story about an enterprising kindergarten teacher in Georgia who was trying to teach her students about geography and maps. She hit upon the idea of asking the children to bring a stuffed animal from home and when they had written their names and addresses and a little message on their animals and attached a little journal, they took them to the airport where they handed them over to pilots and stewardesses who promised to take them on their next flight and then pass them on to other travelers who would do likewise. The idea was for the critters to arrive back home eventually with a list of interesting places they had been.

One little boy said he had sent his very most precious animal who had been with him all his life. That was a breathtaking thing for me to read. My own child, Elizabeth, has a well-worn stuffed animal called Mr. Cat which I handed to her the first moment I laid eyes on her in a dingy government office in Santiago, Chile when I adopted her. The very thought of sending Mr. Cat out into the world on a plane with strangers makes me want to weep. For I know, and you know, the perils he would face, his probable demise in a trash can or lost and found room in some busy impersonal airport far from home. But the child in the newspaper article sent his friend away and trusted that one day he would return.

Few of us expose our most vulnerable selves to that kind of risk, few of us trust the world or other people that much, few of us reveal our secret hearts to anyone - to our dearest friends, to God, even to ourselves.

And yet only by sharing ourselves in some way do we become fully human. In the world of children those little stuffed creatures are their secret hearts made manifest in the world. As adults, our secret hearts are invisible, and for the most part they stay secret all our lives.

On the one hand, there is good reason to guard our secret hearts. What is private is holy, what is personal is deserving of care and cherishing. We don't take off our masks easily for if we did, we would be crushed. On the other hand, too much guarding creates a secret heart that is frozen and inflexible, fearful and stunted. And so, our most secret self waits for the transforming touch of God and for the chance to reveal itself to others and to the world.

Our secret heart is the very core of our being, what theologically we call our soul, and out of that secret heart comes

> the work of our lives,

the love we share with others,

the contribution we make to the world,

our particular reason for being,

our shining presence in the universe.

We are part of the Kingdom, the reign of God which needs our essence to complete the plan, the wonderful dance of time and space of which we are each an integral part. Time spent learning who we are in our secret heart, painful or joyful as we may find that knowledge to be, gives us the courage and strength to move out into the world infused with compassion and ready to love as we have been loved deep within our bodies and souls.

King David found his secret heart a treacherous place. He didn't like what he saw at first, but he knew that if God would only touch it, cleanse it, and restore it, he could go on, he could begin again.

When I was a freshman English major at the University of Georgia everybody had to take biology. Or so I thought. But one day, I discovered that Journalism majors didn't have to take biology; in other words, they didn't have to face the dissection of a frog. They were required to take a lab science but the saving grace was that geology counted. I liked geology. I liked learning about earthquakes and faults and the layers of sediment you can see on the highway where they've blasted through the side of a mountain. So, I promptly changed majors. On such 18-year-old reasoning are careers made.

I especially liked studying rocks and minerals. For instance, do you know what Galina is? Look at the AT&T building up the street sometime - it's shaped like Galina, all cubes and shiny angles. Or what about mica, what we know as fool's gold, that delicate papery layered golden rock. My favorite of all though were geodes. They look like lumps of rough river rock but if you crack them in the middle just right, the two halves fall away and inside is a fairyland of crystal around a hollow core. That interior is carefully and completely hidden from the outside, it is protected, and no one even suspects it is there, unless you are a budding geology student.

Our secret hearts are like geodes. There in the darkness the inner beauty of the geode waits to be revealed by the light. But it has to be broken in two, to be cracked open to be seen in its truth. Because the prophet Nathan pointed King David's secret heart out to him, exposed it to the light, David was forced to look at who he was. And he was shocked. But he also believed he was not a hopeless case. He sensed that his basic value was still intact. Though he knew he had acted out of pride and ego, and though he couldn't look back and find a single moment when he thought he had acted well, and even when he was convinced that he had been bad from the start, in faith he called on God from the darkness for wisdom, for clarity.

But darkness is not all bad. Time spent in the darkness of our souls can be fruitful. The urge to scramble out of the darkness, to put on a happy face, to keep busy, to not let our sad dark feelings show is a negation of the positive comfort of darkness. Allowing others to see some of our darkness can bring comfort and make us feel less alone. It is not easy to spend time in darkness; it is much more cheerful and comfortable in the light. But the darkness has much to teach us. The ability to wait out the darkness, to accept its teaching is a mark of a maturing soul. We need the strength not to succumb to the darkness, to be swallowed up by it, and God will give us that strength. At the same time, we need to learn to be comfortable with living through a dark time without giving in to the temptation to rush its passage.

The paradox is that the very dwelling down in the darkness gives us strength, more than it robs us of it, if we allow it to speak to us, if we allow ourselves to share it with someone else and if we allow God to hold us there even when we cannot see a way out. Even in the darkest darkness we are alive, God loves us, and we are not alone. If we can think of being in the darkness as being held in the arms of God, we can wait and accept the love that container offers. We can think of darkness as a retreat, a time apart for renewal, for healing and after a time we, too can emerge into the light, ready to go on.

Countee Cullen, a poet of our time, knew the value of darkly tending the secret heart.

"The night. whose sable breast relieves the stark,
White stars is no less lovely being dark,
and there are buds that cannot bloom at all
in light, but crumple, piteous, and fall;
So, in the dark we hide the heart that bleeds,
and wait, and tend our agonizing seeds."

Jesus knew darkness - the darkness of loneliness, the darkness of grief, the darkness of despair. But he also knew the value, the goodness of the dark garden where he went with his friends and where he met with and talked with God.

Facing our secret hearts is also like being in a desert, another place with which Jesus was familiar. He faced his fears and temptations there and came to terms with the bare bones of his life, his ministry and his call. "Do not cast me away from your presence, do not take your Holy Spirit from me. Teach me wisdom in my secret heart" says King David. The dark and the desert both seem to speak at first of hopelessness, of loneliness, of fear, of certain death. But as there is goodness and wisdom in the darkness, there is also wisdom and truth in the desert.

My high school marching band was an award-winning group which journeyed far and wide in its pursuit of excellence and large trophies. One football season our school played a team in Tennessee, just across the border from our North Georgia town of Dalton. To get there we passed through Copperhill, a famous mining community. We drove through on the yellow school buses about sundown and I will never forget the stripped red hills as far as the eye could see. There were no trees, no plants, just roads cut in the side of the hills. It was a desert. The bus got very quiet as we looked out at what we pictured the moon must look like (this tells you something about my age for this was before a TV camera gave us actual close up pictures of the lunar landscape.) Copperhill looked bleak, and cold, and dead that day. It crouched among the hills, chimneys sending smoke into the autumn sky, isolated houses huddled on the barren hillsides.

The very ground looked raw as if the skin had been pulled away, the nerves exposed to the light and the biting wind. My young daughter, Elizabeth, calls that tingling, stinging feeling of exposed nerves "spices," that painful, open hurt that begs for the touch of cool water, like the parched desert itself. There are times in our lives when we feel that way, when we have been hurt or have hurt ourselves and every word, thought and gesture expose us to the spice of raw pain. These are the times we medicate ourselves, and drug ourselves into forgetting - not with the cool water of inner growth but with sleeping pills, alcohol or shopping sprees, trashy airport novels, TV soap operas, or sensational but destructive relationships. Our discontent is painted on our faces like red dirt strewn across the rolling stripped hills of Tennessee.

The poet Robert Frost put it this way:

"They cannot scare me with their empty spaces
Between stars - on stars where no human race is.
I have it in me so much nearer home
To scare myself with my own desert places."

There in the desert we are picked clean to the bare bones, purified, cleansed, and ready to see our way more clearly. Alone on a barren hill, exposed to the wind, we wait, vulnerable to the rain and the snow until we have moaned ourselves out and lie exhausted waiting for something new to take hold of us and lift us up.

And the miracle of our lives as Christians is that we can rise to new life, there is a resurrection; we can find our way back to the light and looking around we can see what needs to be done for those in God's creation who need what we have to offer. And like a spiral, in coming closer to God in the darkness and the desert we find ourselves, and we are able then to look to the needs of others, who teach us even more about ourselves and about God. And the cycle begins again.

And in that spiral of growth we find ever more profoundly our individual secret heart, that part of ourselves that is unique and holy and fragile and vulnerable in times of darkness and desert.

That secret heart that we guard and protect so fervently is:

> the same in essence as the secret heart of the person sitting next to us right now,

> the same in essence as the person across the sanctuary,

> the same in essence as the secret heart of the person driving their car past the church - right now –

> the same in essence as the secret heart of the child in Haiti with a raggedy t-shirt hanging off her shoulder as she walks the dusty, garbage filled streets of Port-au-Prince looking for lunch,

> the same in essence as the secret heart of the Rwandan woman whose husband died this morning of cholera in the dusty streets of a refugee camp in Zaire,

> the same in essence as the heart of the richest man in New York City who even as we speak is reading "The New York Times" in a penthouse on Fifth Avenue,

> the same in essence as the secret heart of the Major League Baseball player sleeping late this morning because he had a very long game last night.

We all protect a secret heart and yet all of our secret hearts have a common beat.

> All of us are worried sick that we will be exposed for who we really are,

> all of us pray that someone will really know us and like us anyway,

> all of us seek the mystery of something bigger than

ourselves and some purpose for living,

all of us cry in the night,

all of us look for someone with whom to rejoice.

King David stood alone in a desert of lament, a darkened landscape barren of hope, asking for new life. When he saw what was in his secret heart he asked for a generous spirit and the strength to pick himself up and begin again, to do his job, to govern his people with compassion and justice, to love his family with respect and tenderness.

To see holiness in barrenness, to find sacred possibilities in that which on the surface is only lifeless darkness, to nurture the spark of life which hides itself in rocks and blowing sand, are all hard-won prizes of wisdom. To find value in the apparent worthlessness of a desert calls on our strength of heart and feeling. But to find that holiness and value is to find ourselves and we can go on to find the same value in other people whoever they are and in whatever circumstance we may find them or be found by them.

Our secret hearts learn to wait, to seek and find acceptance; they withdraw and grow and then they reach out for others. We send them into the peril of the darkness like Mr. Cat on a round-the-world journey of unknown destination and we find that he comes home again, battered but enriched by the experience. Our secret hearts are broken in two like geodes and we find the inexpressible beauty and strength they reveal. And underneath the gaping wounds of a strip-mining town there is power and fertility deep in the red earth that will again sustain life.

Where the restless, heavy darkness reveals crystals of hope, there do our secret hearts find wisdom and there do we reach out a hand to those who still walk in the darkness. Where the desert sand meets the bedrock, there do our souls touch the earth of our flesh and we discover our common humanity with all those whom God has created. "Teach me wisdom in my secret heart and sustain in me a generous spirit, O God."

In the name of all that creates us, redeems us and sustains us, Amen.

The Feast of Humanity
Colossians 1:9-17, 25-29

"...the mystery that has been hidden throughout the ages and generations...the riches of the glory of this mystery, which is Christ in you, the hope of glory."

As many of you know, last month I spent three weeks at Princeton Seminary where I'm working on my Doctor of Ministry degree. The group I was with was the same little community I was with last fall. I will spend three more weeks with the same twelve people next summer. It is a varied mix of men and women, black and white. Among us are six Presbyterians, three Catholics, a Lutheran, three Baptists, a Congregationalist and an Episcopalian. All of us are pastors doing our best to be the best we can be and to learn how to do it even better.

My experience at Princeton this summer has started me to thinking about the concept of community. Maybe this is because one of our two faculty leaders at the end of every discussion about every ministry experience somebody brought in, would plaintively ask "where is the community in this? I long to see the community taking part in this experience. Where is your ecclesiology, where is the church, where is the community?" We talk a lot about community around here, too - the Community of Faith, the Caring Community, the Covenant Community. But what is community? That is the question I'll be looking at today.

I am unique in my Princeton community in that I serve the biggest Protestant church represented in our group. Most of the others are solo pastors in churches as small as 70 members and as large as 500 or so. It has occurred to me then that this church, this place, this congregation with its 2400 members, plus several hundred more children plus the 500 people with whom we share this very space on Sunday morning, all added together make about 3500 souls, which is bigger than many small towns. As a matter of fact, on paper, this congregation alone is about the size of the town where I grew up. And look around you today - just in worship attendance this morning - this is more people gathered in one room than inhabit many towns and I wondered about the idea of comparing

The Fire and the Knife

membership in a congregation such as ours to being a citizen of a small town. Each of us has chosen to live in the city, at least for the time being. We don't live in small towns even if we used to. And I don't mean to romanticize small towns - they have their problems certainly, but I want to focus this morning on community and I wonder if we might not get at the concept of community by comparing a large congregation to a small town, comparing a community based on faith to a community based on place.

First of all, there are advantages and disadvantages to living in a small community. To start with, everybody knows who you are. The good part of that for me was that when I rode my bike to town and went in and out of the stores, everybody knew that my Daddy was the one who ran the phone company and if I got in trouble or got hurt, somebody would know who to call. On the other hand, if I was riding my bike up town when I wasn't supposed to be doing that, then word would get back to my Daddy very quickly. Unfortunately, in a congregation of this size we don't know everybody although some know more than others.

Second, in a small town not only does everybody know you but everybody knows your business. The down side of that, of course, is the lack of privacy for the various foibles and sticky situations in your relatives' or in your own day to day life. The up side is that people have a context for thinking about you when disaster befalls. In other words, you have a history, and, in its light, you are thought of as better than the failure you feel like today. Or on the other hand, lest you get the big head about a momentary achievement or triumph, somebody will be there to remember the past for you and will take you down a peg. Again, in a congregation this size, everybody doesn't know everybody's business. We're pretty big on privacy around here. In fact, that's one good reason to move to a city. Some people want anonymity and that's fine but where does that desire dovetail with the concept of community? Can you be in community and be left alone, unknown and unknowing?

Third, small towns always have what is known as "characters," town eccentrics. In the South, at least, these characters are simply accepted as part of the landscape. Nobody feels sorry for them or their families, they just are, they're different. It's the way it is. In a congregation such as this we have our "characters," too. You can identify them yourselves, but the interesting thing is that if we could read each other's minds, we'd see a whole host of "characters" and they wouldn't necessarily be the same ones in every other person's mind! In small towns though, you know exactly who the characters are, and everybody agrees on the list.

One character I remember was actually one step bigger than a town character. He was more like a state character. When I was a child, we'd be riding down the highway with all the windows open on our vacation to see our relatives in South Georgia when Mama would call out, "hey, look, there's the Goat Man." And sure enough an old man with long hair and a beard - in a time when that was actually odd - was sitting on the side of the road with a big cart and a herd of goats, the animals happily eating the grass and trash along the highway. Legend was he was a wealthy man who just liked life on the road and every year he'd go visit his son and get cleaned up and rest for the winter, then he'd start out again in the spring. He was simply part of the landscape of rural Georgia in the 1950's.

But what does this line of thought have to do with Colossians I? And does it get us any closer to understanding community? I'd like to suggest that the idea of community functions in this place in much the same way that the Goat Man had his place in the community which stretched from Toccoa, Georgia to Americus, Georgia. In our text, the Apostle Paul talks about a mystery hidden for generations finally beginning to come to light in the person of Jesus Christ and I'd like to suggest that that hidden treasure is among us even now in the vague, misunderstood, elusive concept of community.

So, the first thing I want to say about community in general then is that you can't really explain it, or put your finger on it, but you know when it's there. Or conversely, as someone said to me recently, "I've been in community before and this isn't it." Community is a feeling, it's an underlying security and strength that can't be described very accurately. And our attempts to categorize it and quantify it are pretty much all in vain. For community changes

like water to ice,

like clouds to rain,

like milk to ice cream,

like popsicles to colored water,

like babies to children to teenagers,

like light to rainbow and back again.

Community is something that you notice once it's there, but you can't truly make it happen. You can try to build it, you can study the idea and do what you can to bring it to be and nurture it, but then it will surprise you by showing up where you weren't even working on it. You can dream about being part of one, but it is most often recognized sometime in the future looking back at it. Community is about people and how they are together, and it is about all the layers underneath the words and the actions and the resolutions and even the picnics and retreats and workshops and meetings. Community is something else altogether and we might as well just face that we can't force it to happen. It's like falling in love: we can only be open to the possibility and alert to its presence and then thank God for the marvelous gift of its coming.

Kathleen Norris is a poet who lives in South Dakota in a very small town. Her book *Dakota: A Spiritual Geography* has made a big impact on me not only because she talks so eloquently about life in small towns but because of her intriguing comparison of life in a small town on the Great Plains to life in a monastery. I read the book late at night for it is calm, and spiritual, and quiet like the wide-open emptiness she describes as her spiritual geography. But for our purposes, at one point in the book, she talks about a trip to New York City, where she had lived previously, to see a friend who was sick.

> "The journey took on the nature of a quest. First, the 125-mile trip over the prairie to the nearest airport, in Bismarck, North Dakota; a plane to Minneapolis and then LaGuardia, where I waited nearly two hours for my baggage; a bus into Manhattan; a taxi to Penn Station, where I stood for another two hours in a vast crowd - it was Labor Day Weekend - waiting for a train. It seemed as if all of the city's dense, humid heat

was concentrated in that room, yet I felt at peace. The crowd was a typical urban mix: all races, young and old, rich and poor, sane and insane, quiet and ranting. As I stood in this group of strangers, I was happy to be one among many, and a powerful calm came over me. I began to see each of us as a treasure bearer, carrying our souls like a great blessing through the world. After the relative emptiness of the Plains, partaking in such a feast of humanity was a blessing in itself."

I am reminded in my own life of a trip to the laser show at Stone Mountain last weekend during the fourth of July festivities. Thousands and thousands of people of all kinds, totally unknown to me but there we all were having staked out our little patch of grass bounded by the borders of our quilt, all of us cheering and singing along and clapping for the American flag and Elvis and the Beatles and the fireworks. Truly mythic, a feast of humanity.

Do you remember the ending of the movie *Places in the Heart?* It was much talked about for at the end of a very realistic and agonizing story about hard times in the Depression in a small town in Texas, the scene suddenly became mystical and magical. There in the church, celebrating communion together in a most unrealistic way, was the whole community, another feast of humanity. There were all the members of the movie's cast, even those who had died during the story along with those who were still alive, those who were enemies and those who loved each other, all together in one community, all sitting together in the pews and the camera focused on each one in turn as the plate of bread was passed from person to person. And something about each person's presence, unrealistic as it was, gave you a really clear picture of the concept of community and the way that each person had a role to play even if it was destructive and not very cozy.

It was a wonderful movie but what I remember almost as well as the ending of the movie was the beginning. During the opening credits and behind beautiful scenes of fields and houses and the people of that small community going about their lives on a Sunday morning was the sound of a small congregation singing "Blessed Assurance." That's a mysterious and mystical hymn about community even if the words are very individualistic. If you change the "I" to "us" and "we" though it makes even better sense today in the context of community.

"Perfect submission all is at rest, we in our savior are happy and blest. Watching and waiting, looking above, filled with God's goodness, lost in God's love."

We're going to sing that song in a few minutes but I'm not quite finished. I am still struggling to get to the heart of this idea of community with you and I can't quite find it. I see community as so much deeper than just being happy about diversity and accepting everybody - whether they're a hand or a foot or an eye or a gall bladder - because that kind of acceptance too easily turns into mere tolerance. And it's one thing to politely tolerate people and their differences but it's another thing altogether to really see, to comprehend, that everybody has a place in a real community. And yet even that suggests action and goals and to me a place in a real community is very different from having skills and talents. For what about the ones among us with no apparent skills or talents? What about people who seem absolutely useless? What about the ones who are simply present? What about the Goat Man in our midst? What about the ones who aren't very bright? What about the ones who are, the ones who are smarter than everybody else? What about the ones with loud unreasonable voices?

I know of a church which was forming a search committee to find a new pastor. They appointed two co-chairs. One was a young woman, an elder, an up and comer, a dynamic, spiritual person who would help lead the church into the next century. And in a stroke of genius and a moment of true community, the church appointed as the other co- chair the church "character," the church eccentric, a man with a deep spirituality but who expressed it in the most outrageous ways. He was intense and off the wall and you never knew what he would say next but together the two co-chairs led the committee to find a pastor who if nothing else got an honest look at the congregation by simply looking at the committee. But even more important, that congregation realized, perhaps unconsciously, that the church eccentric was important to the process of calling a pastor. He was as important to the life of that community as the up and comers. And the balance served them well.

We talk sometimes about our being called to this place, and that's not just the pastors.

Some of us wonder how in the world we wound up here.

Others of us never think about it.

Some of us are here because our grandmothers and great-grandmothers were here and if that is the case, we either feel secure and comfortable in that knowledge. or we feel trapped and constricted like we can never get away from a place where our great-grandparents still people the worship services as part of the communion of the saints.

Some of us are here because somebody down the street invited us to come.

Some of us were channel surfing one morning or one night and for some reason stopped and watched us worship on TV and decided to visit.

Some of us can't remember why we're here. But the fact is that we're here.

Psychologists talk about the idea of projection and how some people just rub us the wrong way and some people draw us like magnets. The point of projection is that not everybody registers on you like that. Most people just move through our lives like water flows through gills on a fish. But when we notice somebody in a negative or a positive way it is because we see some part of ourselves reflected in that person - a part we haven't figured out is part of who we are if we would only claim it. And it has to be the same way with churches. The community holds up a mirror for us each to see who we are, and the community by looking at each of its people is looking in a mirror to see what kind of community it is. There are more than one hundred other Presbyterian churches in the Atlanta area. Some of you ride right past them to get here. Why is that?

The Fire and the Knife

I believe it is because God has carefully designed this place to be peopled by precisely this group of people at this particular time. The basis for community is that we hold certain things in common whether we can identify them or not. You may wonder what part you're supposed to play in this community, but I don't think that's the point. You don't have to do anything to be part of this community. That's what grace is all about and providence and God's unconditional love. We are a group of souls called together by God for a mysterious reason. Our job is to be who we are here and to wait for word on what that means and how we're to go about living out our lives as Christians in a world waiting to hear some Good News for a change.

You belong here because you are here and that is the bottom line - even if you wonder who some of these other people are with their crazy ideas which frustrate you and make you want to scream.

You belong here even if you can't yet find a group within this community that fits who you are.

You belong here even if you feel like an outsider or not good enough or even if you feel you're too good for most of the people here.

You belong here because you are here, and God most definitely had a hand in your coming.

The Apostle Paul said his commission was to make the word of God fully known, to talk about the mystery that has been hidden throughout the ages and generations, and to make known the riches of the glory of this mystery, namely Christ among us. The richness of who we are as a community is largely untapped. The mystery is hidden still. And to me, the mystery is that in Christ all things, including this community, hold together –

whether we understand it or not,

whether we believe it or not,

whether we can evaluate it or not, or explain it, or

disclaim it, or disregard it or discredit it or whole heartedly embrace it. And that is what we hold in common.

The mystery of community is that it is a feast of humanity. God, out of infinite love for creation and humanity, has set the kingdom of God among us in the person of Jesus Christ and Christ's presence is known to us by the even deeper mystery of the Holy Spirit dwelling within each of us and among us altogether in this community. To be one among many, to be a treasure bearer, to carry our souls like a great blessing through the world -that is mysterious and mystical indeed and will take many months of Sundays to try to understand.

What makes each day worth living is knowing about this mystery and wondering how it will be revealed in me and in you and in this place. Look around you. Whether you know it or not, whether you can see it or not, the feast of humanity, the table of grace around which we sit, is exactly as it was meant to be. The First Presbyterian Church of Atlanta is part of the mystery and as Paul said, "may you be made strong with all the strength that comes from this glorious knowledge and power and mystery, and may you be prepared to endure everything with patience, while joyfully giving thanks to God." In the name of all that is holy, Amen.

Floating in Black of Night
Philippians 4:4-6; Isaiah 12:3

"I will trust and not be afraid."

Do you remember the first time you actually floated in the swimming pool or the ocean? Do you remember your mother or your father holding you up and telling you to let go and just float and they were actually going to take their hand away and you were sure you would sink and water would get up your nose? Do you remember though finally the feeling of just breathing and floating, your arms outstretched your back arched while you looked at the sun and your ears filled up with water and your hair floated all around you? To my mind, floating in the water is what Paul was talking about when he said, "do not worry about anything and the peace which surpasses all understanding will guard your heart and mind." It seems so unlikely. It seems so illogical. It doesn't make sense, just like allowing water to hold you up seems absolutely absurd. But it works.

Floaters are not in control. We are vulnerable there on the liquid surface. The ability to relax is essential. I have often thought about floating in the ocean or a dark swimming pool at night and I think of the cruel yet numinous scene in the movie *The Mission* where the priest is strapped to a board like Christ to the cross and sent down the river rapids. There was not a thing he could do to direct his course, to keep from dying; he just floated on the currents, arms outstretched, and plunged over a waterfall to his death.

We don't have to experience vulnerability to the ultimate extent like that priest, and we don't usually have to float in the water but being vulnerable is a state that is part of human life. The capacity to accept that vulnerability and learn from it strengthens us and we learn to contrast the feeling of vulnerability with control. Water at night, dark water is frightening. Not being able to see below the surface, not being able to see a sea creature coming, the sheer terror of not knowing how deep the water is underneath us takes us to a place where we are vulnerable. This mysterious property of water, that it can both uphold us and drown us, the mysterious unseen-ness of dark water as well as its dark warm comfort, can lead us to trust.

That God can uphold us, that God is mysterious and unseen, that God can see us through even a sea of worry only adds to the unexplainable "otherness" that is God.

Paul says, "Rejoice in the Lord always." Another translation for Rejoice is "farewell", a word we use for good-bye, but its old English meaning suggests well-being, traveling with God. To travel with God like a floater on the surface of the water is to live lightly, trustingly, with hope that we will find our way to our destination somehow and that there is a path out of the darkness and into the light. In Advent we are waiting in the darkness for a future that is brighter. We learn trust in that darkness and we experience it every day of our lives when we go with God, when we fare well, when we rejoice in God's power and purpose.

The living water, the well of salvation that we read about in Isaiah is the liquid love that God gives us each day for nourishment and sustenance in the wilderness of life in Advent. At the Lord's table we experience the power of common elements to sustain us in a way that we cannot explain just like we cannot explain why we can float. We know this meal's power in a part of us that we don't understand but somehow, we feel it. The human one who first helped us trust the power in the water in the swimming pool or the ocean showed us with love how to float literally. That one who undergirds our lives shows us again and again with an everlasting love how to float on the vast waters of our souls.

The 14th century Spanish mystic, St. John of the Cross, understood it this way, this ability to float even when worry and disaster swell around us:

"How well I know that flowing spring in black of night.

The eternal fountain is unseen. How well know where she has been in black of night,

I do not know her origin. None. Yet in her all things begin in black of night.

I know that nothing is so fair and earth and firmament

drink there in black of night.

I know that none can wade inside to find her bright bottomless tide in black of night.

Her shining never has a blur; I know that all light comes from her in black of night.

I know her streams converge and swell and nourish people, skies and hell in black of night.

The stream whose birth is in this source I know has a gigantic force in black of night.

The eternal fountain is unseen in living bread that gives us being in black of night.

She calls on humankind to start to drink her water, though in dark, for black is night.

O living fountain that I crave, in bread of life I see her flame in black of night."

In the darkness of Advent, waiting for the light, we float with trusting spirit sustained by a peace that we do not understand, believing that we will not sink into the depths, that we will be upheld by a strong and loving hand.

Rejoice in the Lord, says Paul. Fare well, go with God, accept the mystery and wait with hope for the coming of the Christ child into our souls and into the life of the world. Amen

Clear as Crystal
Revelation 21: 10-11, 22-26, 22:1-20

"And in the Spirit he carried me away to a great, high mountain, and showed me the holy city Jerusalem coming down out of heaven tram God having the glory of God, its radiance like a most rare jewel, like a jasper, clear as crystal...And I saw no temple in the city, for its temple is the Lord God Almighty and the Lamb. And the city has no need of sun or moon to shine upon it, for the glory of God is its light, and its lamp is the Lamb. By its light shall the nations walk; and the kings of the earth shall bring their glory into it, and its gates shall never be shut by day - and there shall be no night there; they shall bring into it the glory and the honor of the nations. Then he showed me the river of the water of life, bright as crystal, flowing from the throne of God and of the Lamb through the middle of the street of the city."

We are deep now into the season of Easter, a time of rejoicing, the most festive time of the church year. This is a time for eagerness and looking forward to the glory that the resurrection represents. No more are we in the season of repentance, although we must constantly confess our shortcomings. Nor are we in the same posture of anticipation that Advent represents. No, now is the time for hope, the time of the foretaste of glory divine.

Picture with me if you will, early morning in a valley on the island of La Gonave, Haiti. The sun strikes the broad leaves of the mango trees and filters through to the rich brown freshly turned soil in the bean and sweet potato fields below. The sunlight is clear, the greens and browns of nature broken suddenly by a procession of people in their Sunday best making their way. through the rich furrows of the fields - the man in a white shirt, his wife in a red dress, balancing a basket of papayas and gourds on her head, two little girls following in gauzy frills, black hair festooned with ribbons and bows. They glide beneath the trees. You can't see it, but you can smell the crisp meat pies frying in makeshift stoves of rusty, dented bowls over small cooking fires nearby. There are sounds of laughter and chattering, shouts of welcome. But it's the early morning light that washes the scene with a radiance that is elemental.

Next shot. Again, it is early morning. The air is cool, the sun

The Fire and the Knife

comes up over a forest in the mountains of Nicaragua. The lake in the clearing is dark blue and the bougainvillea bushes provide red splashes that compete with the colors of the birds flying around the lake. The bird calls echo in the morning stillness and people begin to move through the trees toward the smell of coffee brewing somewhere near. The mist rises from the water and the air is clear with the early morning light.

One more shot. A parking lot in Atlanta, the parking lot behind this church. In fact, it is dawn. The lights of the IBM building are close to being eclipsed by the gray sky. The sun strikes pink and gold the buildings nearby. Shadows move slowly through the morning light. Their faces are not yet recognizable, but their hands are in their pockets against the morning chill. Low voices talk as they move hastily toward their destination. The air is clear. It is peaceful.

"Morning has broken, like the first morning, sweet the rain's new fall sunlit from heaven. like the first dewfall on the first grass. Mine is the sunlight, mine is the morning. God's recreation of the new day."

Such idyllic scenes. Early morning Is s special time of day - its only rival is summer twilight in my view. Early morning when the world wakes up - the world before most of the people.

Our text this morning is from Revelation, that great and glorious dream of John, a vision of the kingdom of God. What strikes me today is the talk about a radiant city, clear as crystal, no need for sun or moon. the glory of God being the light. Rivers of crystal flowing through the city. Jewels are mentioned, too, in the general vicinity of this passage - those sparkling bits of colored light. The book of Revelation is truly the stuff of dreams, hardly believable to us in late 20th century America.

Oh sure, we've seen skyscrapers that glisten and sparkle like jewels.

We've seen golf courses and parks that glitter with dew on emerald grass.

We've seen awesome stained glass, right here in this room and across the hall.

We know the intake of breath when we first look upon a vista of overwhelming beauty and freshness. But the sun rises higher during the day, the dream vaporizes, and we are left with the world as we know it from nine to five.

And behind that first snapshot I envisioned for you of the people in the verdant fields of La Gonave making their way to church early in the morning - behind that scene there is a country which is drowning in poverty. Where the lines of sadness and despair etched on the faces are more plainly seen in the harsh noonday sun.

Behind the lush forest in the mountains of Nicaragua that day, the shadows of the trees harbored contra soldiers with rifles in their hands and killing on their minds.

And behind the sun rising over the jeweled dawn of Midtown Atlanta was a revelation of scores of people in rag tag clothes, their possessions in grocery sacks, led by their bellies to the warm fellowship hall with coffee and grits and eggs abounding.

Dreams can be glorious but as the sun slowly makes its way into the heat of noon, we wake from dreams to see more clearly the world as it really is. Or do we? Is it possible that the light of dawn, clean and clear as crystal, is the reality, and the heat of noon day is somehow a cloak over the glory of God's creation? Is it possible that the early morning light is an image, a symbol of God's true self, a clear and shimmering time that John's dream portrayed for him as a city coming down clear as crystal, radiant like a rare jewel?

Throughout Christian history, light has been a symbol for God. The radiance of clear light has spoken of God's presence particularly in times like the 11th century when stained glass and icons and portraits and other church decoration were forbidden. Churches relied on clear light through clear openings, the play of light on gray stone, the architecture of angles and curves to speak of God's love and care, God's power and majesty. The sun, too, was a symbol for God and it continues to be a powerful force even for the non-

The Fire and the Knife

religious - the sun in its majesty, ever present. giving life to all it strikes, illuminating us and giving us strength.

John Denver said it in 1973.

> "Sunshine on my shoulders makes me happy. Sunshine in my eyes can make me cry. Sunshine on the water looks so lovely. Sunshine almost always makes me high."

But we can't make that special early morning light last. Time marches on. But the feeling of dawn, of dew on flower petals, of sunlight through trees, sunlight sparkling on the water, brings with it a powerful feeling of peace, of rightness, of hope. Surely that feeling is at the heart of God's great plan.

Sallie McFague is a contemporary theologian who is experimenting with some very new ideas. In talking about the symbols we use to talk about God she says that often we fall short of being able to express the intensity of what we feel about God when we are tied to the concept that God is a person, however we picture that person. It is true that we know God as a personal God but there must be other ways to think about God that have more scope. She says

> "certain experiences of ecstasy and awe that cannot be adequately understood in traditional models are more fully expressed in the ocean, the sky and the earth. How might we view the world, she asks, if we were to experiment with the metaphor of the universe as God's body?'

McFague sees the possibility of the world itself providing a meeting place for us with God, just as we have long recognized that in relationships, we are able to see God. But this is not a message about the glorification of nature. Nor is it an environmental sermon. It is a word of peace in turbulent times, for the God of the dawn

> by giving us the clear light of early morning as a quiet place where we can see the way things are meant to be,

by giving us a quiet, still place where we can, in effect, rest in God's lap,

that God of the dawn gives us a space where we can drink in the power and the love and the hope and the peace of creation - and from there go on to our work in the world.

The mystics of the early church talked about the need to empty ourselves, to lose ourselves in the paradox of being made strong in weakness, of losing our souls to find them. And in this way, they said, we can make room for God. In a quiet and open space, we can simply be –

not meditating on God's gifts to us,

not thanking God for our many blessings.

not taking our cares to God,

but just simply draining our minds and just being in the presence of God. In the times when we find it difficult to close our eyes and just be, as a step toward that perfection of contemplation, there is a way to sense through light, clear as crystal, the kingdom of God in all its glory. The essence of that light is God. It is all around us.

The city of God,

clear as crystal,

radiant as jasper,

refreshing as ice water,

is the exhilarating and enchanting dream that was given to John long ago. Our dream of a world that is pure is discouragingly marred by the noonday reality of pain and despair, hopelessness and frustration.

Can we find that place of quiet rest near to the heart of God?

Can we believe in the reality that transcends what we observe from waking to sleeping?

Can we be refreshed in the realm of sleep and the dawn where clear light paints a picture of God that is all too soon erased in the hustle and bustle of our lives?

Yes, we can. God has ennobled us, made us in the divine Image. When we rest in that quiet place, and wait in God's lap, we can see the vision of the kingdom that Easter brings, we can balance our despair with the laughter of sunshine, and we can go forth into the world in hope.

Mistletoe, Mist and Dreams
1 Samuel 3: 2 Thessalonians 1:11- 12

"...asking that our God will make you worthy of his call and will fulfill by his power every good resolve and work of faith..."

Today I want to talk about call. It's a subject that is always on our minds as we seek to do what God wants; but it is on our minds in a particular way these days as it seems to get harder and harder to discern God's will and then even harder still to act it out in the world. First of all, everybody is called. It's not just something absolutely unique that you feel that sends you hurrying off to seminary - although that has been known to happen. Ministers are called but so is everyone - to something. Samuel kept hearing a voice and was sure it was a real person - his teacher in the next room. But it turned out it was God. Unfortunately, that story has fueled our expectations ever since. That was a real call. Samuel actually heard God's voice. Most of us don't feel like we get quite that clear a summons.

On the other hand - the passage from I Thessalonians is about as vague as the Bible gets. It's the other end of the spectrum from Samuel and its guaranteed to intimidate. Paul prays that God will make his hearers worthy of God's call -whatever that means. And he goes on to say if we are worthy of that call, God will fulfill whatever work we are called to by a combination of our good resolve and faith. The amazing thing is that God seems to think that we can hear the call and that then we will act and somehow the work of God will be done.

We all want to have a Samuel experience. But more often what we get is Thessalonians in which case it's all up to us, and that is far scarier than hearing a voice in the night. But yet most of us can attest to some kind of experience where the voice of God seemed clear in a way that it never had before.

Frederick Buechner says the ancient druids took a special interest in in-between things like mistletoe, which is neither quite a plant nor quite a tree, and mist, which is neither quite rain nor quite

The Fire and the Knife

air, and dreams which are neither quite waking nor quite sleep. They believed that in such things as those they were able to glimpse the mystery of two worlds at once. Perhaps in that case, Samuel heard God's voice not quite awake and not quite asleep. It was a message like mistletoe and mist. Like those dreams that mysteriously include a phone ringing and the sound is an actual phone that wakes us up. Was the phone in the dream real?

Hearing the voice of God, recognizing it for what it is and then acting on it is a tricky proposition. Buechner again has this to say about the awesome concept of call:

> "Vocation comes from the Latin vocare, to call, and means the work a person is called to by God. There are all different kinds of voices calling you to all different kinds of work, and the problem is to find out which is the voice of God rather than of Society, say, or the Superego, or Self-interest. By and large, a good rule for finding out is this. The kind of work God usually calls you to is the kind of work (a) that all need most to do and (b) that the world most needs to have done. If you really get a kick out of your work, you've presumably met requirement (a), but if your work is writing TV deodorant commercials, the chances are you've missed requirement (b). On the other hand, if your work is being a doctor in a leper colony, you have probably met requirement (b), but if most of the time you're bored and depressed by it, the chances are you have not only bypassed (a) but probably aren't helping your patients much either. Neither the hair shirt nor the soft berth will do. The place God calls you to is the place where your deep gladness and the world's deep hunger meet."

Mistletoe and mist - it's still not entirely clear. After many years of pondering it - I can buy that God gives each of us certain talents and gifts and puts us in particular places at particular times and what we choose if we are intentional about doing God's will be what we are called to do. But lately I've been thinking more deeply than that. That seems like only the first layer of understanding the concept of call.

I

There are three things I've been thinking about. First, what about when you feel called to something but there's so much about the work that's irritating, discouraging, and bad for your self-esteem - those times we are euphorically called to a work that then slowly turns to mush, that saps more of our energy than it renews? Where does that leave us as called people? I believe God can call us to work that is frustrating but it's one thing to be frustrated and it's another entirely to be totally demoralized. There must have been a reason for the original call - has it served its purpose? Obviously, not every minute of the day can possibly be joyful. There are bureaucratic things that are part of any job. Those are a nuisance, they are housekeeping, they are things that have to be done. Theoretically we can do those on autopilot and get on with the real work.

Even Jesus had to work his way through a crowd. He couldn't be preaching and healing every minute of the day. Although he was lucky enough, he and the disciples, to have a group of ladies accompanying them, acquiring the food and preparing it, setting up the lodging, paying the bills, etc., I guess that was their call. But maybe they wondered, too. Getting the groceries while they knew Jesus was preaching must have been frustrating - especially since they couldn't hear the tape, stream it, or read the printed copy later. Using Buechner's formula - the work made them glad, gave them deep joy and at least from our point of view it was work that God wanted done. Jesus obviously knew his was work worth doing and it gave him great joy - but what about the great pain and the frustration it caused him?

The boy Samuel received a call one night as he tried to sleep. He answered the call and he worried. God's voice told him some bad news about Eli. The Bible says "he lay there until morning." We don't know Samuel's age in this story, but he obviously took a giant step toward growing up that night. He lay there all night. I can see him on his cot, the dim light of the lamp of God near the ark casting shadows, Samuel staring at the ceiling. Time passing. The voice of

God. What would he do with it? The next day he tried to hedge but Eli would have none of it. Samuel told him what God had said although it must have pained him to do it

> The clearest I can discern, call has to do with opportunity. Have you ever met somebody who was the right person at the right time and you fell together as friends with little effort and felt as if you'd known each other forever? Shirley MacLaine would say you had known them forever. But when that happens to me, I have enough experience to realize that this is a person sent for a reason, and it is the beginning of who knows how long an association for who knows what reason. And when the times get tough, I think back on the meeting of these two souls and trace the thread of where we were, and where it led us. It was a call albeit a maddening one. Like chess - you make one move that might not make sense in the short run in order to be in position for the one down the road. The catch is you can't see what's down the road. Only God can do that. It's mistletoe and mist.

II

So on to the second question. Can there be more than one call, more than one overarching "purpose" for your individual life? When I grow up, I'm going to be a doctor, says my daughter Elizabeth. Maybe she will, maybe she won't. But if she does, and is a very good doctor, could she be called to something entirely different after she's been a doctor for a while? Of course, she could.

But as grownups we know how hard it is to shift gears so momentously. We need a clear call indeed from God to make that kind of a change! Abraham did it. He was a farmer and then he uprooted his family and became a wanderer. Jesus was a carpenter and then he was called to be a preacher and healer. Granted, he was special - but even for a human in his thirties who lived in a small town, it must have been just a little hard to strike out along the lake, leaving his workshop not to mention his family behind.

Used to be you worked for the same company your whole career. My father was a telephone man. He started by climbing poles and rose through the ranks with the same company to district manager status and then he retired. But now one career can last for just a few years then an entirely different one can begin. Sometimes the shift is caused by the times - job layoffs, obsolete industries. Sometimes it's a growing interest in another area, or the discovery of a total mismatch of talents. Sometimes it's a growing conviction that God wants us to do something different, to move in a different direction. But how do we know? That's the core of the dilemma. Mistletoe and mist.

III

Which leads me to the third question - is there a call within a call - are we enabled somehow through one call to pay serious attention to another one at the same time? Does our first call somehow give us the energy and time to pay attention to a further call that is maybe more important? And that is where my struggle lies. Sort of like the old joke about the optimistic boy who kept asking for a pony and when on Christmas day he found a living room full of horse manure said "there must be a pony in here somewhere!" This is not to say that the primary work is not valid. We are involved here in work that is important, work to which we feel called. Granted it is work that is not the same as working in a leper colony, or feeding homeless people at 6:30am week in and week out down by Grady Hospital. But perhaps this kind of work enables us to do some of that other kind of work, or at least to contemplate doing other kinds of work that God needs doing but that we haven't reached clarity on yet.

There is something stirring around inside me right now that needs doing, that needs me to do it. I can't see it very clearly, but it is like a fugue. I do the work I do now to one tune but there's this other melody playing underneath that I can't identify. As Carl Jung said, there's gold down there in the darkness. Mistletoe and mist. Sometimes in dreams I am doing it, the work I can't identify. But when I'm awake I'm left with music that I can't place or repeat, and it drives me crazy.

Now these are all very important but luxurious questions. It is wonderful and heady for those of us with the means and the intelligence and the support to be able to consider these questions.

The Fire and the Knife

But what about for people, say, on the island of La Gonave, Haiti or in a village in the mountains of Nicaragua or in a refugee camp in Africa?

How do you even feel a call when most of the time you are preoccupied with what you're going to eat for supper?

How can you tell what God wants you to do other than keep your child from dying before she's two?

How can you home in on your life's work if you can never even look up from the hoe in your little bean field that no matter how hard you work it, still won't feed your family?

On the other hand, it sometimes seems easier for those with less, to more clearly see what God is calling them to do. It is irrefutable that the people in churches in Africa, in Haiti and in Nicaragua are more joyous and animated in their worship than we are and more generous relatively speaking in giving to those who need what little they have to give. I saw it myself in Haiti when they took up the offering - people giving coins for others when they had so few for themselves.

There's a novel I love called *The Bean Trees* by Barbara Kingsolver. In it a young woman is determined to do two things - get out of rural Kentucky and not get pregnant. She changes her name from Missy to Taylor, buys an old VW and heads west. She's not sure where she's going but her car breaks down in Oklahoma. As she finally begins her westward trek again a woman comes over to the car and hands her a child. "Please take this baby," she says and walks way. Suddenly Taylor is a mother. She was on the way somewhere else when she was called to do this other thing. She felt called to Arizona (as it happened) but she was handed another call at the same time. If she hadn't been on the way west, she wouldn't have been handed that child. In making a life for herself in Arizona, she's making a home for a child. To which did God call her? It's messy being a mother; it's messy working as Taylor does at a car fix-it place called Jesus is Lord Used Tires. She never knew she'd be called to first be a waitress and then a tire changer and she never expected to have to make a living and a home for somebody else.

Which was she called to - one thing or all of them? It's mistletoe and mist. Not just one thing and not just the other.

Paul says by good resolve and faith we answer God's leading and respond to a call. Samuel, feeling foolish, said "Speak for your servant is listening" and the Lord came and stood there and spoke to him.

The notion of call is not tied to a time or a place or an activity. God's time and places are not ours, but God breaks into ours with an urgency that can't be denied. It can't be denied because it is compelling - either over time, and we finally break down and respond - or it's compelling in its vagueness, the haunting melody we write in our sleep that we can't recall the next day, the dreams of not quite waking or sleeping call to us. There are things that are plants but not plants, rain but not rain. We are left with a notion, a clue, and God surely leads us to a better understanding and action - not necessarily in that order.

But maybe this is all too technical, too small. Maybe it is simply part of being human to be constantly looking for something, to ache to find something that will unwind the crumpled paper bag feeling in our souls, something that will enable us to feel fulfilled, to feel that we are doing what we were set here to do.

> "We search for a self to be", says Frederick Buechner. "We search for work to do. And since even when to one degree or another we find these things, we find also that there is still something crucial missing which we have not found. We search for that unfound thing, too, even though we do not know its name or where it is to be found or even if it is to be found at all."

Mistletoe, mist and dreams - clues, hope, mystery. It is the call of the Christian. It is the life that God has given us. Thanks be to God. Amen.

Let the Little Children Come
Mark 10:13-16

"...and he took them up in his arms, laid his hands on them, and blessed them."

This little story that is our scripture for this great occasion is just that - a little story. Jesus is taking a break one day and some little kids come to talk to him. And the disciples know Jesus is busy, he's tired and they try to keep the kids away. But Jesus hears about it and says it's OK. He likes kids. He's rejuvenated somehow by them. They're messy, yes, sometimes they talk too much - but all in all, they are magical and fresh and new.

There's a story about a little girl whose baby brother was kept in a bassinet in her mother's room and because the parents feared sibling rivalry, etc. they wouldn't let her near the baby. She kept begging and begging and finally they agreed. Then the little girl said she had to see him all by herself. The parents agreed to stand outside the bedroom doorway as she met her baby brother for the first time. She approached the bassinet and leaned over, peering at him carefully. Then her parents heard her loud whisper to him. "Kevin, what is God like? I've almost forgotten."

That's a little story, too, like the one the Bible tells us today. And I tend to think the Bible story is really true. For why would it be recorded otherwise. There's no great miracle or stirring sermon that Jesus preached. No cataclysmic event in his life. It was just a day like any other and this happened, and we are told of it. Possibly the punch line about the kingdom of God is the main point the writer is trying to make but it is set in an everyday context that probably happened more than once. It is a story - once upon a time some children came to see Jesus.

Frederick Buechner, a Presbyterian writer greatly popular among Presbyterian ministers, has written about stories such as the one we are told today. Here's what he says ...

"... this is what Christianity is. If we whittle away long enough, it is a story that we come to at last. And if we take even the fanciest and most metaphysical kind of theologian or preacher and keep on questioning him or her far enough - why is this so? All right, but why is that so? Yes, but how do we know that it's so - even that theologian is forced finally to take off the spectacles and push the books off to one side and say "once upon a time there was ..." and then everybody leans forward a little and starts to listen .... The Storyteller's claim is that life has meaning - that the things that happen to people happen not by accident like leaves being blown off a tree by the wind but that there is order and purpose deep down behind them or inside them and that they are leading us not just anywhere but somewhere. The power of stories is that they are telling us that life adds up somehow, that life itself is like a story. And this grips us and fascinates us because of the feeling it gives us that if there's meaning in any life - in Hamlet's, in Mary's, in Christ's - then there is meaning also in our lives. And if this is true, it is of enormous significance in itself, and it makes us listen to the storyteller with great intensity because in this way all the stories are about us and because it is always possible that the storyteller may give us some clue as to what the meaning of our lives is."

So Buechner leads us back to our Bible story and to our story today. Once upon a time some children came to Jesus and he was eager to talk with them, to hug them, to love them. Once upon a time, a man and a woman had a baby and they loved it and they wanted the best for it and they brought that baby to Jesus Christ for they sensed that Jesus would welcome their baby. And indeed, he does.

God in Christ welcomes us all into the household of faith with love and hope and grace, not because of anything we do or are but because of what we desire to do and who we desire to be. Let the children come to me, said Jesus and today we come with a child. Katie Blake, who today we baptize, is a real child, a new child, the symbol of all our hopes about life. But again, according to Frederick Buechner,

> "... we're also all of us children still. No matter how forgotten or neglected, there is a child in all of us who is not just willing to believe in the possibility that maybe fairy tales are true after all but who is to some degree in touch with that truth. You pull the shade on the snow falling, white on white, and the child comes to life for a moment. There is a fragrance in the air, a certain passage of a song, an old photograph falling out from the pages of a book, the sound of somebody's voice in the hall that makes your heart leap and fills your eyes with tears .... and whenever you find tears in your eyes, especially unexpected tears, it is well to pay the closest attention. They're not only telling you something about the secret of who you are, but often God is speaking to you through them of the mystery of where you have come from and is summoning you to where you should go to next."

Buechner calls us to pay attention to the child within us. Jesus calls us to pay attention to the children among us. A real child, the symbol of trust and innocence, of a direct connection with God - calls us to remember who we are and whose we are in the great and continuing story of life. Once upon a time some people gathered to welcome a child into the household of God and together they remembered their own childhood, their own baptism and they clung with joy to the mystery of God.

The River of Life
Genesis 49:1, 29-50:3; Matthew 24:38-44

*"Gather around, that I may tell you what will
happen to you in days to come."*

Most of us have seen that old bumper sticker - In case of the rapture, driver may disappear. Of course, the humor is underlain by the shock value, but I submit to you today that even if it's not the rapture, people disappear all the time and it is very hard to deal with it. And I'm not just talking about death.

If we had a choice most of us would probably want to be like Jacob also known as Israel. "I'm about to die," he says to his son Joseph. "Here are instructions about what to do with me." Then he dies quietly at the end of many years and most of Egypt seems to go with him to the interment - quite a send-off.

On the other hand, some of us might prefer for ourselves the way Jesus outlines for the coming of the Son of Man.

Two people on a picnic, one is taken, one is left behind.

Two people at a movie, one is taken, one is left behind.

Two people on a golf course, one is taken, one is left behind.

The Bible says it will happen that way. But in the meantime, we live with good-byes - sudden or expected - and the old cliché about it being toughest on the one left behind, is, of course, the point of it all. That's the way life is, that is the only way we have to live.

And the depth of the tragedy,

    the enormity of the feelings of abandonment,

        the subtleties of being bereft are as mysterious as the disappearances in our lives.

The Fire and the Knife

Two couples are in a car accident and three out of the four die leaving two children orphans, two more fatherless. The one survivor without husband and two best friends must face the rest of her life with their memories. Or taking it out of the realm of death, two friends build a relationship of trust and fun and mutual support and one day one of them simply refuses to speak to the other anymore and there is no explanation, just a deafening silence.

Bewilderment springs to mind. It's hard not to take it personally. It's one thing to die quickly or slowly - whatever your preference. It's another to be left behind suddenly. And like a sentence you diagram in high school English class, there are branches, forks in the road for every kind of abandonment. Subtle turns, blinding flashes, burning, missing, dull ache. And sometimes they happen to us in a tumble. It's not just one person a year and you adjust to it. It's several in one week. Or one this week that dredges up the memory of somebody who left years ago.

I had a computer consultant at the church where I work who was wonderful. He seemed to know everything there was to know about Macintosh and IBM and all the software ever written and how to hook up this machine to that one. And not only all that, he was fun. We laughed, we compared notes on lots of things, we had lunch. I had a list of stuff to ask David the next time he came. Unfortunately, I still have that list on my desk because David died last month in a motorcycle wreck. He stood at the bottom of the stairs up to the second floor the Friday before and talked to me about a computer problem I was having. We chatted for a while. And now he's dead – D-E-A-D - dead.

But people die all the time. I didn't know David very well. We were just getting started on a professional intermittent relationship, but we connected and now he's gone. He didn't abandon me on purpose. And his family no doubt was far more deeply saddened and stunned by his death than I am but something about it won't let go of me. People die that I knew only vaguely, and I think that's too bad, or I am genuinely sad for a while but it's the unreality of somebody practically vanishing that just doesn't fit. It makes you want to reach out literally to the friend closest by and hold on to them for dear life for fear that it could happen to them on the way home that very day. People in earthquake land must feel similar unreality. The ground, the very earth we live on betrays them one morning as they're dreaming and shifts violently, and they run outside into the dawn and listen to the unearthly roaring and wonder what they can count on if not the ground they're standing on.

Who can you count on if they can go to lunch and simply not come back?

I think you have to count on the river of life itself. The rage, the grief is very real, and they are all that counts when you're feeling them but beyond that, the river of life keeps sending water, new water, new energy that takes the form of individual people that come into our lives and then leave. We make plans, but they are not life's plans. We hope to live happily ever after and die at a ripe old age with our family and friends around us, but life may not have that in mind. So, what is the point?

The point is, I believe, to live with integrity in relationship with those whom God places in our path right now. My path and your path cross right now but they won't run parallel forever. We are pilgrims with destinations known only to God. What goes on in the depth of the souls of the people around us is known only to them and to God. If I could draw a graph of my life it would have ups and downs, but it would run on a linear course. Here is where I was born, here is where I am now. But when I try to overlay that graph with the graphs of everybody I know, I can only find the tiny intersecting point of our lives now at this moment - no more. I can't see where they will end up any more than I can see where I will.

At this point it would be easy to be discouraged and anxious. We are tempted to chain our children to our wrists so at least if we are taken, we think they will be, too. But that also thwarts the river of life which goes where it wants to. I remember the scene in the movie "Out of Africa" when Meryl Streep is trying to get the workers on the coffee farm to damn up the river and make a pond to irrigate the coffee plants. Her African friend says it won't work because "this water lives in Mombasa." And sure enough when the first big rain comes, all the sand bags are washed away and Streep throws up her hands and says "don't try to stop it. This water lives in Mombasa."

We damn up our days by trying to hold back the river of life. We try to protect the people we love. Even if we don't mind the idea of dying ourselves and may even look forward to the adventure, we definitely don't want to suffer the loss of our families and friends, and we try our best by various mental incantations and bargains with God to keep our near and dear near and dear. We are clear that we're in it together and by being close to each other for however short a time, we find ourselves closer to God.

The water lives at Mombasa. It flows right by us sometimes. It flows right over us sometimes. And sometimes we are in it flowing right by other people. Our consolation is that someday we will know as we are known and one day,

we'll be able to ask the why's,

we'll be able to reconnect,

we'll see for ourselves how the whole plan is laid out.

But until that day we hurt when we lose someone, however they leave us, and we ache to see faces that are gone. At that point we plunge our faces into the cool water and feel the energy of the river of life, knowing that it is clean and pure and has a destination that we can trust.

We can be here today and gone tomorrow. We don't know what will happen. What we do know is that God is here today and tomorrow directing the river's course and offering us consolation and security in the person of Jesus Christ who brought us together for today and sends us forth into tomorrow.

Most of us who grew up in the church were taught that our souls, our minds, were what counted and that our bodies were just the housing for the all-important soul. After all, when we die, our bodies return to dust, but our souls are eternal. But to be human is to be housed in a body. Jesus was. God became flesh and dwelt among us. And so, our bodies are as important as any other facet of our being. "They need not go away; you give them something to eat," says Jesus. But it goes beyond family night suppers and food pantry bags, even beyond prayer and worship. I think Jesus meant that along with giving people what they need spiritually that we are also to honor people in all aspects of their lives - including their senses and their human physical forms.

Our Run for Mission every year helps people in need, but it also honors the fact that we can run and walk, our bodies have strength and power.

Our church picnics are about fellowship, but they are also about food and playing out of doors.

Our Vacation Bible School is about teaching children about the faith, but it is also about our human physical need and ability to paint and draw, and glue and paste, and create with our hands and see with our eyes.

And likewise, this table before us is about eternal life, and remembering Jesus, but it is also about eating and drinking, about smelling and tasting. This is our spiritual food, but it is also our physical food. Often, we lose sight at the Lord's Supper of the fact that it was an actual meal that people shared. They had more to eat that night than little bits of bread and a tiny glass full of wine. We need not be so quick to dismiss the tangible aspects in order to get to and ponder the spiritual aspects of this meal

Jesus directed us to care for people's souls and our own, and he also said "you give them something to eat," "honor your own bodies and its needs." We need the nourishment of the love and grace of God which we were enabled to see and experience in the human life of Jesus Christ and which we continue to see and experience in our own very human lives. But we also need the physical nourishment of food, food that has a smell and a taste, that we can see and touch here at this table and beyond. We are body and soul together, thanks be to God.

Finding Our Way Home
Acts 2:41-47

"They broke bread from house to house and ate their food with glad and generous hearts."

The idea of home, of a place where we belong, where, as Robert Frost said, if you must go there, they have to take you in, is one that occupies us throughout our lives. If we are lucky, we knew what home meant as children. We were safe and warm and loved there, and we spend our adulthood trying to duplicate it. If we were not so lucky as children and had to survive abuse or dysfunction or if we were orphans and the people taking care of us did only a minimal job, then we knew what home was only vaguely and we continue to try to find it as adults where we have at least a little more power to make it happen.

Home is an illusory concept, a mystical place. John Denver says he was born in the summer of his 27th year, going home to a place he'd never been before. Cowboys said home was a place where never was heard a discouraging word. Conventional wisdom says home is where your heart is. And everybody from Perry Como to Dolly Parton has warbled that there's no place like home for the holidays, a sentiment that inspires everything from tears to hoots of scorn from listeners every year. Our story, this glimpse of the New Testament church in Acts, tells us about a concept of home that has nothing to do with your family of origin.

In fact, Old Testament scholar Walter Brueggemann has pointed out that while the Old Testament's idea of home was a group of relatives headed up by a man, usually an old one, who decided who went where when, in the New Testament, family, home, community was a group of likeminded individuals that were probably not related to each other at all except as brothers and sisters in Christ.

As far as I can tell, those people in Acts didn't all live together. We have evidence that they ate together and spent time at the temple together but not that they lived in a kind of commune. Maybe some did. But it was the times they came together that they were at home in a strange new kind of way. The New Testament people in Acts spent a lot of time at the temple and then they ate "from house to house," kind of like a Biblical progressive dinner. They liked each other. They ate their food with glad and generous hearts. Sounds like the spaghetti dinner scene in "The Big Chill". We probably all can point to a time when we first felt at home outside our families of origin.

For me it was my first quarter in college. I had associated myself with the Wesley Foundation, the Methodist center at the University of Georgia. Being a good Southern Presbyterian 18-year-old girl, I had dutifully trudged over there my first Sunday in Athens and just kept going back. We watched "Sesame Street" and "Mr. Rogers" in the afternoons – both shows brand new in the late 60's - then went to dinner at the dining hall. On Wednesday night we had a meeting during which we planned our coffee house program for the weekend.

I can never remember the name of that place, but our specialty was Hot Dr. Pepper, an incredible concoction involving boiling Doctor Pepper with lemon slices floating in it. We all sipped it sophisticatedly while somebody played George Harrison's song "Something" on the guitar on a little stage in an old house. It was the "in" place to be at the University for a while. Somebody did astrological readings in the back room (lit by a black light and a lava lamp, of course) and we lived for those intimate, warm nights together in the turbulent early 70's.

This idea of home as unrelated people who love and accept each other is a liberating one for single people. Single people have a hard time with the concept of home. Where is your home when you are 35 and not married and don't live in the house you grew up in or even in the house where your mother and/or father live today? That home can be a place where you are accepted as you are by people you are not related to, is a wonderful idea. In 1979 in my 20's I rented an apartment in Little Five Points. The first night I was there was exciting, moving boxes around, shoving the little bits of furniture against the walls, carefully constructing and arranging the board and concrete block bookcases. But when I turned off the light and lay down on the Macy's mattress set right on the floor I cried and cried. I was terrified. For the first time in my life

> I was not living with my parents,
>
> I was not living in a dorm,
>
> I was not living in an apartment with friends.

Was I home? Not by a long shot.

So, in trying to define home - a difficult thing to do if you get past blood relatives - I have come to the belief that home is that place where you feel safe and warm and loved. It's hard to feel safe in our world. I don't know how men feel, but women go through life rarely feeling entirely safe. Hardly a day goes by when some danger or the possibility of one doesn't stare you in the face. You always have to be on the lookout. And safe is relative, but if you can find a place that at least feels safe you are a big chunk of the way home. Warmth is also a part of being home. It implies relaxation. So along with safe, you have to be warm, you have to be able to relax to be at home. Which brings us to the hardest part of all - home as where you are loved.

> Orphans can be warm and even safe but wonder sometimes about being loved.
>
> Abused children can be warm but not safe and certainly not loved.
>
> Adults can more easily control being safe and warm, but we all search for love outside ourselves.

And though it's wonderful to have another specific person there to love us, sometimes that isn't the way the cards are dealt - whether we're single or married for that matter. But we still need it and never give up looking for it.

Presbyterian minister and psychotherapist Ann Ulanov gives us a clue to this search for home when she says that by seizing an outer truth, we can find our way to an inner one. We've talked about feeling safe and warm and loved in the world but somehow

> home is deeper than locks and keys though somebody's arms around you in protection is very attractive,

> home is more than warmth and relaxation though there's nothing like a quiet afternoon by the fire with somebody you love,

> home is more than being loved by somebody else though many would argue that the whole exercise of loving and being loved is what life is all about.

No, the inner truth which is the true concept of home is one that Whitney Houston unwittingly sings about when she says

"Where do broken hearts go
When they find their way home?
Back to the open arms
of the one who's waiting there."

Back to the open arms of the one who's waiting there. In the end, that can only be God.

But lest you sigh in disappointment that now I'm going to leave hugs and crackling fires for the abstract concept of God's being our ultimate home listen to Ann Ulanov again.

> "God's presence emerges in concrete situations and particular lives, not in abstract generalization or rhetorical labels in which persons do not really exist at all. The pattern of discovery is of a God who remains veiled even when unveiled, [but who is also] a being who loses no mystery by becoming accessible. Probing being in its concreteness takes us further and further into the presence of mystery, a presence that does not lend itself to verbal statement but only summons us to receive it in concrete experience."

With open arms God receives the broken-hearted just as we walk into the accepting arms of another human person. But which came first for us as human beings in the pursuit of home - the chicken or the egg, the inner experience of God as our true home or home as we find it or make it in the outer world? God is surely present in those people we call family, or in those unrelated people who care about us and ask about our lives, who hold us literally when we are afraid or sad or thrilled to death. They are God at hand when we are needy and we can carry the memory of that literal feeling of hands and arms and voices when we go inside ourselves to commune with God, our true home. It's a circle, there is no first or second.

There are those who have not yet experienced home in an external or an inner sense and they look on skeptically when we describe the experience. But God can find them, too, through us. For how else can we know the peace, the safety, the warmth that is God without having experienced it in our lives somewhere.? And as we have received, so we can pass it on.

God is home,

> we are home to others,

>> others represent home to us

and they lead us down into ourselves where God is at home waiting for us. As Paul Simon says in his song "Homeward Bound" – "home, where my music's playing, home, with my thoughts escaping, home, where my love lies waiting silently for me."

And that description holds true on an outer level as we go through our lives sustained by other people as well as when we go inside ourselves to the dark and inviting place that is God in each of us –

> where music is playing,

>> where our thoughts escape,

>>> where love lies waiting silently for us.

We can find our way back home. God will lead us to someone who will represent safety and warmth and love and through whose love we can find our way back to God. It's impossible to predict when it will happen or what form of human being or beings it will take. But there is a home for all of us on earth as well as deep inside ourselves. The two homes sing to each other and draw us into themselves. They feed us as humans and as souls. I wish home wasn't so hard to find. But those moments when we actually catch a glimpse of it, we know without a doubt that we're really there.

Landscapes and Highways
Acts 9:1-9

"...get up and enter the city, and you will be told what you are to do."

I think we can all look at our lives and recite what has happened to us and most of us do it by naming important events.

In 1969 I graduated from high school.

In 1973 I graduated from college.

In 1979 I graduated from seminary.

In 1983 I was ordained.

In 1989 - a big year - I started working at this church and my daughter, Elizabeth, came home from Chile.

In 1994 I was accepted at Princeton for their D. Min. program.

There are other important dates, too, more private ones with months and days of the month that I will never forget, and I always mark them when they come around again.

Paul surely marked the year of his life, and the month and day when Jesus became his personal lord and savior, the day on the highway that the bright light came from heaven and his friends heard a voice but saw nothing. Paul was a busy man. He was breathing threats and fired up about stopping those pesky Christians and I can almost see him trucking down the road to Damascus that day, intent on getting there. He was carrying a letter and he was bound and determined to catch a few of those who were part of a movement called The Way - men or women, didn't matter, Paul was hot on their trail.

And so, when the incident happened on the highway that left him blind and with no appetite for three days, it was surely marked in his chronology of adulthood and we know he whipped it out at every opportunity and told it with great embellishment in the years that followed.

We're like that, too, I think, intent on the road, running with our eyes on the ground in front of us. The road was important, and you had to be able to see the curves and turns. There was one of those silly songs that was popular way back in my teenage years that went "Keep your mind on your driving, keep your hands on the wheel, keep your snoopy eyes on the road ahead. We're having fun, sitting in the back seat, hugging and a kissing with Fred." The moral of that song was to keep soldiering on, mind your own business, do what you're supposed to do and don't pay attention to what's going on around you.

Well, I have a problem with that, ever since I read a quote from somebody named Ernest Schactel who John Patton quoted in one of the never-ending lists of books I'm reading for Princeton. The wise Mr. Schactel said that "adult memory reflects life as a road with occasional signposts and milestones rather than as the landscape through which this road has led." "Adult memory reflects life as a road with occasional signposts and milestones rather than as the landscape through which this road has led. When I read that I wondered how I was guilty of that and how life and memory would be different if I could try to be aware of the landscape instead of just the highway. How do you remember the landscape, or better yet how do you pay attention to the landscape as you go along so that when you look back there's something other than the date that you remember?

This week the University of Georgia Alumni magazine arrived, and they had decided to focus on the events of the spring of 1970, twenty-five years ago. Now quick, what happened to you in the spring of 1970? Got it? It was very easy for me to recall. The spring of 1970 at the University of Georgia was a time of turmoil at a Southern party school trying to get on board the anti-Vietnam War band wagon. I arrived there in the fall of 1969 when girls couldn't go outside the dorm in shorts and we had a 10pm curfew on weeknights. My dorm room was on the ground floor in the back and since the windows could be opened, I had a constant stream of girls

The Fire and the Knife

climbing over me in the middle of the night trying to sneak in past the housemother. This was all to begin to change that day in the spring of 1970 when the National Guardsmen shot the students at Kent State University.

Hundreds of us immediately marched in outrage to the Academic building that night and then marched onward to the president's house where we sat down in his front yard, a beautifully landscaped formal garden full of boxwoods bathed in light reflecting on the Southern mansion with white columns and a long porch. It was a fine spring evening, and nobody wanted to study for finals. The president came out on that long porch with a bullhorn and said the police were going to arrest anyone who wouldn't leave and go back to campus. Well, we left and promptly marched home. The phones rang off the wall with mothers and fathers calling to tell us to stay out of trouble and not to get around those crazy hippies.

That's how I remember that week. But the UGA magazine gave me some background I didn't know or had forgotten. There were pictures of people who wrote the articles now and from the yearbook 25 years ago. It was funny. I recognized several of the faces and more than one of the names. It was a fine time to be in college.

So, I remember Kent State, but I like to think I remember the surrounding events, too. It makes for a better memory. There was a whole new era in the making. There were dramatic changes going on in the culture and in my own little late teenage life. That same Spring, I was falling in love with a boy who liked Barbara Streisand and the Carpenters. He was so cute. Unfortunately, he died in a car accident in 1983, long after we graduated and went our separate ways. We never had the chance to work through our split and the changes he, particularly, underwent. He was part of the landscape of 1970, not directly related to the Vietnam War and Kent State but part of that whole time for me. I think his draft number was 354 so he was in no danger there.

Things happen to us and we easily remember the date. But things are going on all around us. Paying attention to the landscape adds a certain richness to events, puts the time of our solitary lives into perspective. I am probably most tunnel-visioned on the events six years ago last week when I met Elizabeth for the first time as a three-year-old in a dusty bureaucratic building in Santiago, Chile. I read her my journal from that time recently and it's full of my fatigue and her busyness, my frustration and her wonder and discovery. What I forgot though is that there was a dictatorship still in control of Chile when we were there. Everybody was afraid. The cab drivers had hair trigger tempers. I had to be careful. When I think of her first three years there as having been lived in an atmosphere of terror and grief and secrets and shadows and gunfire in the night, it makes the week I spent there with its dates and signposts much smaller. And it makes my experience, the fact that I got all the legal work done in one week, all the more extraordinary.

The apostle Paul was blinded to all but what was happening to him. Did he start paying attention to the landscape after his revolutionary dateable event on the road to Damascus? I don't know. But we can. Often though the problem is our sense of duty and obligation, commitment and responsibility. The very words sound heavy and force our necks down into an angle that can only see the road and not the landscape. But I think there is a difference

>between doing our duty and living an abundant life,

>>between obligation and wonder,

>>>between commitments to anyone or anything and living our own lives, the lives we were created to live.

Sometimes you have to get off the road to see the landscape. Last year when I was in Northern Scotland on the island of Iona we went for a walk to the far side of the island - about three miles. When it came time to come home, we decided to take a shortcut. It was snowing, and I was carrying a video camera bag and tripod. The shortcut took us across a bog and every step filled my boots with freezing water. Finally, we figured out that if we followed the sheep tracks, we'd at least stay out of the water even if it didn't prove to be a straight shot back to civilization, namely dry clothes and a hot cup of tea in front of a fire. The tracks meandered up and down, backtracking over and over, but eventually taking us where we wanted to go. By leaving the main road we saw parts of Iona that people don't usually see.

But there is a danger both in leaving the road and in staying on it. On the one hand if you leave the road you might never get anywhere. On the other hand, if you stick to the beaten path you never know the wonders of what lies beyond the asphalt. Paul was intently following the highway when a bright light forced him to go by another way. When we are willing to give up control as Paul did, blinded and shocked, a whole new life can await us. We can be part of the landscape, taking it all in and living lives full of awe and creativity. When we are seeing the landscape instead of the highway, we can get lost, but we can also find our lives.

Jesus is Lord of the landscape, the Way with a capital W, a way that leads not in expected directions or straight dependable lines. Nor does it always stick to duties and obligations. But it is all the richer for the risk that following it can bring.

Paul, by changing from a focus on the reliable highway to a focus on a vulnerable journey through a treacherous landscape, finally found the road toward the self he was created to be. Our own highways lead through landscapes we have been afraid to explore. That God leads the way no matter where we go is our faith and our hope. Our past is as much evidence of this adventure as the unseen future will prove it yet again. Thanks be to God!

Behind the Curtain
Hebrews 6:19

"We have this hope, a sure and steadfast anchor of the soul, a hope that enters the inner shrine behind the curtain, where Jesus, a forerunner on our behalf, has entered…"

Toward the end of the movie of the *Wizard of Oz*, Dorothy's dog, Toto, reveals an old man behind a curtain pushing buttons frantically, talking into a megaphone and scurrying around to maintain the illusion he has created of himself as the great and powerful Wizard of Oz. Dorothy, who has been cringing before the wizard because he holds the power to send her home again, is suddenly empowered when she finds the wizard to really be the simple old gatekeeper at the Wizard's palace.

"You're a very bad man," she tells him furiously disappointed. "No, I'm a very good man, dear, just a very bad wizard," he tells her contritely in the movie's most truthful moment. And he further reveals that while the wizard had devised all kinds of tests before he would tell Dorothy how to go home again, in fact, he had no idea whatsoever how to get her back to Kansas.

Every one of us can think back to a time in our lives when someone practically walked on water and then one day disappointed us. Perhaps it was our father or our mother; maybe a special teacher or coach, or a beloved minister. Perhaps it was our first love, or our favorite uncle. But somehow in the end he or she let us down, showed us for the first but not the last time, that perfection is not part of our character and that even the best of the best cannot be more than human.

By the same token, chances are we ourselves have disappointed someone else along the way who thought we walked on water until one day, and we may not even know it, we sank like a stone in their eyes.

We are all less than God. But God is God and in Hebrews we are told that the One we worship in front of the curtain is the same One behind the curtain. "We have this hope, a sure and steadfast anchor of the soul, a hope that enters the inner shrine behind the curtain, where Jesus has entered." We approach with our breath held, our hope a fragile dandelion and slowly draw the curtain aside. And to our amazement and relief, we are not disappointed - Jesus is waiting there, the other side of God.

What this verse - which by the way, I can't remember ever having read before - what this verse says to me is true on two levels. One is internal, the other is interpersonal.

When we talk about human beings like the Wizard of Oz behind the curtain, like we ourselves who we see in front of the curtain, we are talking about the psychological concept of persona. Persona is the mask we wear to operate in our daily lives. Everybody has one. Some people have more than one, different masks for different situations. And a persona is necessary. Kind of like sunscreen. Our true self, our inner person is delicate and in progress. Our true self isn't fully formed yet, and it must be protected from all but the most intimate of friends and family. And sometimes we even protect our true selves from them. God knows our true self and God is often the only one who does.

And furthermore, even we don't always know our true self. It lies deep inside us waiting for attention, waiting to be recognized in a painful process. Sometimes we get glimpses of it in moments of greatness or courage, in service to others, in dreams. Sometimes we get a hard look at it in moments of failure or in the eyes of someone whom we have disappointed. Sometimes we don't like what we see; sometimes we are pleasantly surprised. It is easy to believe in our persona, to pretend we are that one we present to the world; we construct a personality that is acceptable to others; we get by.

But one day we realize that we are not living our true lives. We're pleasing somebody else. We're going along year after year being who our parents want us to be or being the one who seems to be the most successful. But eventually we stop ourselves and turn around and conclude that life isn't worth living unless we are being who God created us to be, our true selves. We look behind the curtain, we test the aching tooth with the tip of our tongues, we hope that what we find will be acceptable to ourselves, to others and to God.

If we can face this truth, that who we are behind the curtain is who we really are and that that person is acceptable to God and ultimately to ourselves and also to others, then we can transfer that insight into our relationships with others. We can search for the person behind the curtain in everyone we have to deal with.

> The obnoxious colleague,
>> the irritating person on the other end of the phone line,
>>> the frustrating person we must collaborate with because it is our job,

is displaying a persona that is the fragile barrier between the self and the world that enables that person to get through the day. Most of us assume our true selves will be rejected. We bury who we really are behind bluster and loud opinions because we would be wounded if we walked around exposed.

It is a hard thing indeed to trust our true selves to anybody on the front side of the curtain. But we do. We pick out one person or a few and we slowly begin to reveal who we really are. We put out feelers, opinions, and see how they are received. If favorably, we try another one, a little more daring, a little more radical maybe. At some point, it's too much and we hurt somebody, or get hurt ourselves. The curtain is torn, it falls off the curtain rod a bit like those shower curtain rings that rip through the plastic after so many trips from open to closed, or one too many tugs from a child holding on to it to get out of the slippery tub. So, we pull the curtain firmly shut again and wait a while to try again.

But the good news of the gospel is twofold in this case. Jesus the Christ is waiting with us behind the curtain, guarding our most holy and true selves from harm in general but helping us to pull the curtain aside not only to begin to truly live as free beings because Christ is within us, but also to face those outside the curtain.

And from the other point of view, Jesus the Christ is waiting with us as we watch somebody else go through the painful process of pulling the curtain aside to reveal himself or herself in all their glory. And when the curtain snags for them, we can look at them with the eyes of love knowing the risk they are taking, having taken it ourselves and we can reach out to accept the other persona, true self and all, for we ourselves have also been accepted as well.

To stand in front of the curtain patiently waiting for someone else to emerge is the business of love.

To stand behind it and open it as someone waits outside for us is the work of courage. God grant us the love and the courage to be truly human on both sides of the curtain.

The Good Treasure
Lamentations 3:19-26; II Timothy 1:1-14

"I remind you to rekindle the gift of God that is within you…guard the good treasure entrusted to you…"

We don't spend a lot of time with Lamentations, preferring the cheerier parts of the Bible, the more obvious Good News of the New Testament. The closest we come is the Psalms or maybe the major prophets like Isaiah and Jeremiah especially at Christmas or Easter. And of course, we like the Bible stories about the great heroes among the patriarchs and matriarchs. II Timothy is also a neglected book. It's somewhere toward the back of the Bible, after the gospels and before Revelation. But both of these books have much to say to us and as is often the case with lectionary readings for the day, they echo each other, speaking to themes that are common not only to the passages themselves but also to our interior and exterior lives.

Lamentations is complicated book and a clever one. But we often miss not only the carefully constructed literary devices the Hebrew writer uses but also the poetry of the book for, in fact, the scholars say the book is three poems expressing grief over the destruction of the temple in Jerusalem and the subsequent exile of the people. In Hebrew this book is called 'ekah, translated How? In other words, the writer is mystified over how God could let this happen,

    this exile,

        this humiliation,

            this grief,

                this homelessness

which the people felt so intensely.

II Timothy is from the second century of the Christian church and is a letter about endurance in the face of suffering written by one person to another. The people in this case had expected the end times to come, for Jesus to have returned sooner rather than later but it hadn't happened, and they were getting discouraged. Throughout both books though, glimpses of encouragement shine through what feels like the brick wall of frustration that makes up our daily lives.

For we usually can't see through the fog to tomorrow and we can't tell if we're just stumbling along in the dark headed toward a cliff or off into the woods full of poison ivy or if we're extraordinarily lucky, straight down the "right" path. I was reading a murder mystery not long ago about a woman alone in an unfamiliar house who, of course, was stumbling around in the dark because she heard a sound. Why she didn't call 911 and hide under the covers is beyond me but no, she got up to investigate. Some intuition guided her as she walked in the complete darkness and the same intuition stopped her just short of what turned out to be a staircase leading down into an unfinished basement.

And that's how we feel, too, sometimes not being able to see two steps ahead of our faces and desperately convinced that we're headed in the wrong direction. On a less literal and more metaphorical level, I've always been haunted by the Robert Frost poem "The Road Not Taken." It has always spoken to me of the sheer panic of choosing wrongly and winding up somewhere I shouldn't and don't want to be, of having made a bad decision and finding myself somewhere on the other side of the world from where God really wanted me to end up. And how could I ever make it right? How could I make it back to that wrong turn? I hate the idea of backtracking; it galls me to think of doing things twice, wasting time, losing momentum but how to avoid it?

"The thought of my affliction and my homelessness is wormwood and gall! My soul continually thinks of it and is bowed down within me," says the writer of Lamentations. And the writer of II Timothy seems to be answering the lament when he says "I remind you to rekindle the gift of God that is within you. God did not give us a spirit of cowardice but of power." In other words, don't despair, the answer is within you. Your soul has the answer. Your soul has the key. Lamentations echoes this idea of an inner source by saying "it is good that a soul should wait quietly for salvation." Well that's the last thing I want to hear. Wait quietly, rekindle the gift within you? How does that tell me how to walk in the dark? I need to get up and make a few right decisions, a few mid-course corrections and get on with the journey. "Guard the good treasure," says II Timothy's writer. What good treasure? and again, How? Which brings us full circle back to Lamentations 'ekah - "how!"

I found a measure of relief from the anxiety-provoking verse of Robert Frost in the haunting verse of a contemporary Welsh writer named Ruth Bidgood. She may or may not have read Mr. Frost's tormenting poem, but she has her own version of his riddle, her own version of the journey. Listen to her poem "Roads":

"No need to wonder what heron-haunted lake
lay in the other valley
or regret the songs in the forest
I chose not to traverse.
No need to ask where other roads might have led,
since they led elsewhere;
for nowhere but this here and how
is my true destination.
The river is gentle in the soft evening,
and all the steps of my life have brought me home."

Now that is good news. I feel my soul stir and relax on that gentle river; I feel my spirit soar like the heron above that unseen lake. My heart sings its songs in a deep quiet inner forest. I feel my mind unravel from the endless strip of agonized theorizing about how my life could have been if I had only gone a different way.

When I was small, I used to ask my mother what it would be like if I had a different father. She would always laugh and answer "you wouldn't be you" but I couldn't imagine that. I was me and I couldn't see how I could ever be anybody different no matter who my parents were. And in some ways, I believe I was right. But in any case,

I do have the parents I have,

I have made the decisions I have made,

I did walk the paths I chose for myself and here's the miracle - all of them are right. All of them are leading my soul exactly where it needs to be.

The people I see, the places I go, the home I have made is the only one that counts, the only life I could have fashioned because it is the one I fashioned, and it is my home. My journey is my journey and it is the gentle river of my soul's choosing. The writer of Lamentations sounds a brief note of hope. "I call this to mind and therefore I have hope - the steadfast love of God never ends, it is new each morning. Great is thy faithfulness." And 2 Timothy's author joins the chorus hundreds of years later saying, "Guard the good treasure entrusted to you with the help of the Holy Spirit living in you."

The Good Treasure, this knowledge that our souls know where they are headed, is a gift. And a Welsh poet handed it back to me, rekindled it in me when she proclaimed in clear and baptized triumph "nowhere but this here and now is my true destination - all the steps of my life have brought me home."

The people of Israel lamented and wondered how to survive their exile. They waited, and it came to pass all in good time. The early Christians were fading in their enthusiasm because Jesus was not coming quickly enough. All they could do was to blow softly on the embers of their souls to rekindle the good treasure of the Holy Spirit glowing within them.

In Ireland in days gone by, the women would put peat on the fire at night to protect the precious coals in the darkness and then in the morning they would take it away and rekindle the flame for the day's needs. The embers burn red and warm within us, too, this good treasure of the soul waiting and being instead of acting and doing. There is a time for acting and there is a time for waiting. The good treasure is within us here and now. It is our home.

As a Christian community, our home is the table spread before us. In the cup glows the warm welcome, and in the bread the fragrant enfolding in the arms of a loving God. Jesus Christ is with us all the time even when we thought he was away for an indeterminate time. Gathered around this table we tell each other by our presence that for now, here is where we need to be. Our souls have heeded God's call and we have measured our steps, we have followed the gentle river and we have reached this holy place.

Thanks be to God.

The Little Guy
Luke 19:1-10

"...hurry and come down; for I must stay at your house today."

This week in the newspaper there was a full-page spread size photograph of the 1995 World Series Champion Atlanta Braves. There in all their splendor were the players, the coaches, the bat boys, everybody but Ted Turner himself. What I liked best though was the back row. Lined up were David Justice, Mark Wohlers, Steve Avery and right in the middle of the row was Mark Lemke. He's standing beside Justice a whole head shorter than the famous right fielder. He's grinning like crazy. If you watch baseball at all you know that Lemke is from Maine, that he has two false front teeth, he always looks like he needs a shave, but boy can that little guy play second base. He's the shortest member of the team (along with Belliard and Maddux) but on the back row in the photograph it was more than obvious that he is considerably shorter than the majestic David Justice who is well over six feet tall.

Our New Testament lesson today is the familiar story of Zacchaeus, the little guy who had to climb a tree to see Jesus in a parade. People in the Middle East in Bible Times probably weren't that tall anyway, so Zacchaeus must have been really short. Nevertheless, he climbed up there and before he knew what was happening, Jesus had stopped and declared that he was going to Zacchaeus' house that day for lunch. And the Bible says, "Zacchaeus hurried down and was happy to welcome him."

The Psalm of the morning - 119 - is the longest Psalm at 176 verses. Today's section has to do with justice, no pun intended. At one point we read "I am small before you and of little significance, yet I do not forget your commandments". And at another point "I am indignant and angry for my enemies forget your words." The writer is looking for a world where justice and order prevail, where God's decrees are honored, and where everybody appreciates that righteousness. Alas, that world is hard to find.

The Fire and the Knife

Zacchaeus was a tax collector; a sort of IRS auditor and he was not well liked. But Jesus points out to the crowd that Zacchaeus is as much a child of Abraham, a member of the local Jewish synagogue, as they are. Jesus always had a way of turning the prevailing order upside down. Jesus called to the little guy, the little guy accepted, and Jesus proclaimed his salvation. The one who was lost was found. We don't know how Zacchaeus felt about his profession, we don't know how he felt about the people who whined and griped about him. What we do know is that when singled out of the crowd he enthusiastically answered the call of Jesus and was willing to entertain him and welcome him on short notice.

"I am small before you and of little significance," says the Psalmist in the face of Almighty God and God's eternal order of justice and righteousness. And at the end of the reading the writer asks for understanding that he may live. It's as if Zacchaeus himself is speaking in the Psalm. His struggle with his job and his faith are evident between and within the lines.

What then do Mark Lemke, Zacchaeus, and this chunk of the Bible's longest Psalm have to say to us today as we try to welcome Jesus into our lives and abide by God's rules? How can we live with the tension between, on the one hand, "trouble and distress have come upon me" and on the other hand "your commandments are my delight"?

Well, I think we have to begin by saying that life is always a paradox. There are tensions we are forced to hold and never resolve. There are situations that have no satisfactory outcome. There are relationships that are mixed blessings, there are jobs that have aggravations and joys, there are churches which are full of people who drive us crazy and people who we thank God every day that we have as friends. With our eyes set on the idea

> that God is good,
>
> that God's judgments are upright,
>
> that God is present always in perfect faithfulness,

The Fire and the Knife

that we are never going to be perfect

and that God loves us anyway,

then from there it is far less of a climb to try to see over the heads of those we either revere or fear. Zacchaeus went out of his way to see Jesus but in the end, Jesus saw him.

I think about Mark Lemke who day after day, six months a year, stands out at second base waiting to do his job. I think about all those years he's tried and failed along with his teammates to catch the gold ring, to catch a glimpse of glory and this year he made it. I think of Mark Lemke on the back row of the team picture peering over the shoulders of much taller men to see the photographer. I think of him grinning like crazy, fresh from a ride on top of a fire truck and I think of myself trying to do what I do struggling to understand a little better every day how I am supposed to live my life.

When we think the scales are weighted against us for one reason or another, we can take comfort in Zacchaeus and Mark Lemke. If we despair that we're

too short or too tall,

not smart enough or too smart,

not faithful enough or too impatient,

too anxious, or too picky,

we can remember that God chooses us for reasons that don't make human sense.

Mark Lemke is no less a member of the Atlanta Braves because he's not six feet tall and Zacchaeus was not any less a member of the Jewish people because he had an unpopular occupation. And you and I are no less a part of the household of the Christian faith even though we sometimes fall flat on our faces in defeat and humiliation.

When the joyful moments come, we can try to be thankful and mindful of what is happening so that when the frustrating times come, we can remember regular people sometimes finish first. All of us at one time or another have been singled out of the crowd. And all of us are summoned to meet Jesus face to face - even if we're the shortest and least worthy one on the team.

At this table, like Zacchaeus, we are happy to welcome Jesus into our lives, into our very bodies as we struggle through the paradoxes of living out our faith in an uncertain and perplexing world. This has always been true, it is true today and it will always be true, thanks be to God.

Snow Village
Isaiah 2:1-4

"Many peoples shall come and say, 'come, let us go up to the mountain of the Lord, to the house of the God of Jacob; that he may teach us his ways and that we may walk in his paths.'"

A couple of years ago I began collecting a line of ceramic pieces called Snow Village. These are those little buildings and houses you see under Christmas trees or on mantels or if you're a real fanatic, filling a whole room of your house. There are also lines called Dickens Village, Heritage Village, Lilliput Village and Christmas in the City. Snow Village though is small town America. When you set up the pieces and turn on the lights that light them up inside and add trees and cars and people and get right down close to it and drink it in, it's amazing the feeling you get. So far, I have the courthouse, a library, a hospital, a couple of stores, a church and a couple of houses.

It doesn't take much self-analysis to see that I am trying to recreate the town where I grew up in the 50's. Of course, there was rarely snow at Christmas in Toccoa, GA but we fervently wished there was and that's the point of Snow Village. Fantasy. Pretty harmless if you have the money. And even if you don't, you can take part in this little village phenomenon by admiring other peoples' collections.

Elizabeth and l aren't too picky about sticking to the Snow Village party line. We're not purists. If Eckerd's has a little house for sale that's about the right size, we'll buy that for less than the investment required for Snow Village. The same goes for little trees and traffic cops and stop signs.

We're creating a little world that we can imagine being in and living happily ever after.

We can make it just like we want it.

We can imagine what it's like to live there.

The Fire and the Knife

We can leave out the bad parts and just remember or create the good parts.

But guess what! Snow Village really exists. It's a town called Celebration and it's in Florida, 15 miles from Disney World. No snow there, of course, but listen to these reports from a newspaper article and from Time magazine about this actual model town being built out in the middle of nowhere. "A new American town of Fourth of July parades and school bake sales...spaghetti dinners and fireflies in a jar...clean-cut, all-American, orderly, safe, quaint gingerbread houses fronting tree-lined streets, porches and picket fences, shaded sidewalks, small parks, a model school, a church, a grassy area with trees, a big flagpole, a library and a cemetery." They've thought of everything.

And you can live there if you win a drawing for a place in either an apartment with the rental price of $650 per month or in a house of your own, the design of which you can choose starting at $128,000. More than 250,000 people have inquired about this town before it's even been built. Ultimately 20,000 people will live there. Disney believes that "the public's appetite for the wholesome surroundings they've created at Disney World is limitless. By offering good schools, clean streets and grass around the edges, Disney is creating a fantasy world so far removed from common experience that people are amazed at the prospect "

Sounds like quite a place and I'm not knocking it. For one thing I own stock in the Walt Disney Company and for another I would like to live in a presumably safe place like that. But I wonder how they're going to control such a place? How are they going to control ordinary, imperfect people and the ways they choose to live their lives? The other side of human nature can't help but be present behind the picture windows even though there will be a homeowners' association that will not let you

hang clothes on a line in the front yard,

paint your house purple,

put your junk car up on blocks on the front lawn or

put the front seat of an old pickup truck on the front porch for your neighbors to sit on while they chat with you of a summer's evening.

To further illustrate this idea of the dark side, the other side of a perfect, pretty picture, on the actual other side of the page in Time magazine where I read about Celebration Florida there is the horrifying story I know you saw about the criminals who killed a woman in order to take her unborn child so they could have a baby, too. What if they had enough money and wanted to move to Celebration, Florida? Are they going to check criminal records?

And not nearly that horrifying an example of inhumanity and human cruelty, but the kind of thing not planned into Celebration, Florida or Snow Village for that matter, is the story from South Carolina last week of a 13-year-old boy who hijacked his school bus demanding to go to Georgia. He was brandishing his father's handgun which he had hidden in his violin case. The bus driver said she didn't have enough gas to go to Georgia and the boy surrendered. Who's going to screen his family from Celebration? Will there be a regulation against handguns? Or will there be a requirement that every home have a handgun?

Our cynicism about life will not let us fully believe in either Celebration, Florida or Snow Village. But that's not the point. We're not alone and this is nothing new. I imagine the Hebrew people thousands of years ago said much the same things and presented the same kind of evidence to Isaiah when he described the glorified Jerusalem of our text this morning. "The mountain of the Lord's house will be established, and people will stream to it. They will beat their swords into plowshares and their spears into pruning hooks. Nation shall not lift up sword against nation, neither shall they learn war any more." Sure. Tell that to the people of Bosnia.

But after all, it's Christmas Eve.

This is the night when a baby is born in a stable who will save the world.

This is the night when a teenage unwed mother will give birth to a baby who will redeem all the people.

This is a baby born in a shelter surrounded by farm animals.

This is a child who will be king of the universe. Sure.

Cynicism aside, the point is, the Good News is, the bottom line is that the table before us, the Lord's table, is open to all who, despite the evidence, hold out hope of a glorified Jerusalem, hope in the possibility of the existence of Snow Village, hope in the prospect for success of Celebration, Florida. The truth is that this meal before us is a meal for those who would love to live in any of those places and who try to live their lives as if they already do. This is a supper for those who really do look to the mountain of the Lord which promises peace. Jesus invites us here no matter who we are - no matter if we want to paint our house purple or if we like pickup truck seats on the front porch, or if we want to see sheets waving in the breeze in the front yard.

It is also a table for those of us who want to live in an immaculate gingerbread house where everything has a place, for those of us who want to park our car in the back in order for the street out front to look tidy, for those of us who want our children to be well-behaved and to do well in a model school. It is a table and a feast for the people who want to live in Celebration but who don't have $120,000 and for those who have $120 million.

This is a table that is for real life and it is also a table for what is not yet real but which we believe will surely be. That is the definition of the Kingdom of God. And it begins again tonight when a baby whose family couldn't afford Snow Village, much less Celebration, is born again in our hearts. So, come to this table those with much faith and those who would like to have more; those who have been here often and those who have not been for a long time, those who have tried to follow Jesus and those who have failed. For it is the child of peace born this night who invites us to meet him here this morning. Thanks be to God!

Testing God
Exodus 17:1-7

"...the Israelites quarreled and tested the Lord, saying 'Is the Lord among us or not?'"

Well, weren't those children of Israel a whiny bunch? Here they are rescued from Egyptian slavery, led by the hand across the desert wastes for forty years with enough food for the journey provided from the sky, a fearless leader, a community moving together under God's guidance and here they come one hot afternoon whining for water.

But look again. Why shouldn't they ask for water? Jesus did. It was the first thing out of his mouth when he met the Samaritan woman - "Give me a drink." The Israelites were just a pre-echo of Jesus - "Give us water to drink," they said loudly and clearly. We don't need to rehash the human need for water and its necessity for our very survival. We need it. It's simple. Without it, we die. And so, the Israelites were only trying to stay alive. Then why did Moses take such offense?

Well, I think it was because he was afraid. He didn't have any idea where he was going either. And he feared the people's anger. He thought they were going to kill him, and he didn't have a clue where to get water in that barren and desolate place. Luckily, he remembered again to consult with God, who basically sighed and said go on out there ahead of the group and strike a certain rock and I'll be there, and you'll have water. Been there, done that. Another miracle for an untrusting leader.

I just can't get away from this picture of a whole lot of people and animals milling around in the desert with sweaty dusty faces, babies crying, children pushing each other around, grownups verbally sniping at each other and Moses and Aaron standing off a ways whispering and listening and looking up at the sky and then hitting a rock with a stick and water gushes out. You can also imagine the mad rush for that opened hydrant. You'd think that after all the plagues and the Red Sea and the manna the people would get it that

God was present on this journey. But all that's easily forgotten when you're thirsty and desperate.

I keep asking myself how long Moses would have waited to try to find water himself on this incredible journey. Maybe Moses thought they got thirsty too soon. After all, he was busy trying to read the map and figure out what to do next. It's like being lost on a country road and trying to read the map on the straight stretches and the air conditioner's broken and you're hungry and your child has to go to the bathroom right now.

On the other hand, you would think Moses could know in advance that people have to have water, even more so out in the desert. After all, they'd just left a real nice oasis with seventy palm trees and twelve springs of water. So how come he didn't take a bunch of skins full of water with him from the oasis? Sounds like poor planning to me. Well, I'm sure they did but they had probably used it up long ago or somebody spilled it and Moses, bless his heart, to give him credit, believed somehow that God would come through again but the bickering and the moaning in the heat of the sun just got to him and he started arguing with them. And they pushed back and suddenly he was in real danger.

And so, God stepped in. Go over there, I'll be waiting, hit the rock, voila, water. And so it was. Can you hear the chaos in this story, the frustration, the longing, the panic, the anger, the exasperation, the indignation, the anxiety, the pain, the feeling of abandonment and desertion, the lack of faith? This crowd was a bundle of nerves and I guess I would be, too, after forty years in the wilderness, a cross-country backpacking trip that never ends.

It reminds me of those times when I was in college and we'd set out for the distant beach on a Friday afternoon and only when it was too late would we try to find a motel for the night. Common sense told us to stop when it was about nine o'clock, but we pushed on. Then at ten all we saw were No Vacancy signs, at eleven it was hopeless, but we kept on going, a little farther, a little farther until it was after midnight, and still we couldn't find a place. Finally, we kept on driving and eventually got to the beach with no sleep and feeling gritty and dirty. The frustration of our plans going awry was enough to make us sit down and cry.

Well, the children of Israel knew more than the leader in this case to my mind. "We want water," they said, "and we want it now." And God answered them because of course, they had a right to water. And God wanted them to live. But what if they had killed Moses and Aaron in frustration? What then?

Would they have all died because nobody would know what to do?

Would another leader arise, or would they somehow have to figure out a way to approach God themselves?

Surely, they had the experience to know that in the past Moses had talked to God, had beseeched God, had listened to God and God had provided. Would they have figured out that they were no different than Moses, that God is approachable directly, that God knew they had to have nourishment? After all, they were only human.

Some would say that they weren't ready spiritually to approach God on their own. But everything that has happened in the Bible up to this point says that's false. God appears to whomever God chooses, the unlikeliest of people. Think about Abraham and Sarah or Hagar and Ishmael. They didn't need a mediator or somebody with an MBA, or an M. Div. for that matter! But ah, it's so convenient when somebody else is responsible for leading you to God. That way if they fail, you can blame it on them, you're not responsible. But if you must deal with God yourself, you're responsible for your own communication with the divine one and your own growth in faith.

Moses, the fearless leader, unbeknownst to the people of Israel, was not going to guide them into the promised land. Yes, he had a few tasks to go before they got there, namely the Ten Commandments and the golden calf, and the tabernacle. But they would have to make it to the land of milk and honey by their own ingenuity and their own faith. They would have to touch the divine with their own souls without Moses to help them out.

Moses showed them how it was done and then he left it to them to take up where he left off. Moses didn't always have the answer; he wasn't perfect - he couldn't find water in a distracting and frustrating situation. Later on, he let his anger get away with him coming down from the mountain and finding a roaring party in progress. He didn't always want to listen to or wait for God. He went one step forward and two steps back just like any other human. But he got the journey going and showed them how to proceed. And for that, all the generations that came after him called him great.

It's hard to know how to proceed on a journey or in a new direction when you've never done it before. But if you can watch it being done right you can do it, too, haltingly at first, to be sure, but gradually with remembered hints and your own improvements and techniques, the legacy of dealing with God from the depths of your own soul is passed along to you for your time and your place.

We can only hope that we have got the hang of it well enough as we set out on our own. Living water, water springing from a rock, is there for the taking, a gift of God freely given. God knows we need it. We only have to ask.

Bibliography

I have always been a voracious and wide-ranging reader. In these sermons I often quote books, newspapers, movies, poems and songs. In a sermon a preacher quotes those writers she needs to illustrate points of the sermon. There is no way to "preach" a footnote, so I have decided to list the books and poets that I reference in the sermons but not page numbers from the sources. The rest of the references beyond books and poets can be found in popular culture. The reader will also note that these literary and cultural references come from the years prior to the 21st century when I left the First Presbyterian Church of Atlanta.

Bidgood, Ruth. *Selected Poems*. Seren Books, 1993.

Buechner, Frederick, *Wishful Thinking; A Theological ABC*. Harper & Row, 1973.

Buechner, Frederick, *The Magnificent Defeat*. HarperSanFrancisco, 1985.

Buechner, Frederick, *Whistling- in the Dark: An ABC Theologized*. Harper & Row, 1988.

Calvin, John. *Institutes of the Christian Religion*. Westminster John Knox Press, 1993.

Frost, Robert. *The Poetry of Robert Frost*. Holt, Rinehart and Winston, 1969.

Kingsolver, Barbara. *The Bean Trees*. Harpercollins, 1989.

Lee, Harper. *To Kill a Mockingbird*. J.B Lippincott Company, 1960.

McCourt, Frank. *Angela's Ashes*. Scribner, 1999.

McFague, Sallie. *The Body of God: An Ecological Theology*. Fortress Press, 1993.

Norris, Kathleen. *Dakota: A Spiritual Geography*, Houghton Mifflin, 1993.

Raine, Kathleen. *Living with Mystery: Poems 1987-91*. Golgonooza Press, 1992.

Schmemann, Alexander. *Introduction to Liturgical Theology*. SVS Press, 1966.

Sloyan, Gerard. *John: Interpretation: A Bible Commentary for Teaching and Preaching*. John Knox Press, 1987.

Ulanov, Ann Belford. *Receiving Woman: Studies in the Psychology and Theology of the Feminine*, Westminster Press, 1981.

www.ingramcontent.com/pod-product-compliance
Lightning Source LLC
Chambersburg PA
CBHW052136110526
44591CB00012B/1748